THE PURSUIT OF TRUTH

PREVIOUSLY BY MARK HICHENS

Wives of the Kings of England: From Hanover to Windsor

Prime Ministers' Wives

Oscar Wilde's Last Chance: The Dreyfus Connection

The Inimitable P.G. Wodehouse

Queens and Empresses

Women of Consequence

The Great Performers

Abdication: The Rise and Fall of Edward VIII

The Great Entertainers

THE PURSUIT OF TRUTH

MARK HICHENS

EDINBURGH

First published in Great Britain in 2018 by
Off The Press Books

www.offthepressbooks.com

e-book available

Copyright © Mark Hichens

The right of Mark Hichens to be identified as the author of this work has been asserted by him in accordance with the Copyright, Design and Patents Act 1988.

All rights reserved. No part of this publication may be reproduced, transmitted, or stored in a retrieval system, in any form or by any means, without permission in writing from the publisher, nor be otherwise circulated in any form of binding or cover other than that in which it is published and without a similar condition being imposed on the subsequent purchaser.

Typeset in Times

ISBN 978-1-9164092-1-7

Front jacket shows, clockwise from top left:

BERTRAND RUSSELL / Bridgeman Images
LEO TOLSTOY (b/w photo), Russian Photographer (20th century) / Private Collection / Bridgeman Images
GEORGE ORWELL, c.1949 / CSU Archives / Everett Collection / Bridgeman Images
CHARLES ROBERT DARWIN

*To the memory of William Tyndale (sometimes Hychyns) –
of all writers of English the greatest.*

CONTENTS

Foreword	ix
William Tyndale	1
Jean-Jacques Rousseau	13
Thomas Paine	19
Charles Darwin	33
Karl Marx	45
Henrik Ibsen	51
Leo Tolstoy	57
Bertrand Russell	65
George Orwell	75
Jean-Paul Sartre	95
Alexander Solzhenitsyn	101
Index	117

FOREWORD

Mark Hichens was first led to write this book when he discovered that William Tyndale, one of the greatest writers of the English language, assumed for a time the name of Hychyns. Why is not known, but there might be a connection to his own, and he was eager to find out all that he could about William Tyndale and what followed from him.

Christ before Pilate. 'What is truth?'

William Tyndale – portrait / Lebrecht Authors

Bridgeman Images

WILLIAM TYNDALE

(1494—1536)

ARCHITECT OF THE ENGLISH LANGUAGE

In 1609 in the reign of King James I, there occurred an event which was to prove of historic importance. The king ordered a new translation of the Bible into English. Since the break with Rome in the fifteen thirties there had been several of these, but it was felt that another was needed which would embrace as many as possible of the different Protestant orders. And so fifty-four scholars were assembled and entrusted with the task. For five years they worked at it, and in 1611 there appeared the King James Bible, better known as the Authorised Version which many consider the most influential work of literature of all time. Millions of copies were to be sold all over the world in over seven hundred languages and tongues. It was believed then to have been a joint effort with no individual predominating, but later when the matter was examined closely it was found that the publication was almost entirely the translation of William Tyndale in 1534.

Like William Shakespeare, the other literary giant of the time, little is known for certain of Tyndale's family background and early life. It has been discovered that the Tyndale family came from the north of England and moved south into Gloucestershire at the end of the 15th century. Why the family did so is not known, but one can speculate. At that time England was in the throes of the long protracted civil war known as The Wars of the Roses, and in 1461 the bloodiest battle England had known was fought at Towton in Yorkshire, resulting in an overwhelming victory for the White Rose of York. Perhaps the Tyndale family found itself on the wrong side in the wrong place and made the move south out of danger, at the same time changing its name to Hutchins (or a near variant). In the gentle slopes of the Cotswolds the family was to do well for itself, perhaps in farming or in the cloth and wool trade for which the district was renowned.

The date of Tyndale's birth is estimated as being 1494, and it is likely that at first he would have gone to a local grammar school where he did well enough to be sent into Oxford at the age of twelve to Magdalen College school (of which Thomas Wolsey had once been headmaster) and then on to Magdalen College, founded in 1458 by William Waynflete and where the famous Tower had just been completed on which a choir ever since has been welcoming the dawn of May Morning. (It should be noted that when Tyndale was entered into Magdalen at the age of fourteen it was as William Hychyns by which name he was to be known during his time at Oxford and for some time after.) Oxford at that time consisted of twelve colleges with about a thousand pupils and was the leading university in England if not in Europe. Subjects would have been mainly Greek and Latin, and most teaching would have been spoken, books being still comparatively rare. Tyndale was to stay twelve terms in Magdalen, and when he took his degree in 1512 at the age of eighteen there is little evidence of his having gained any great distinction. For a time afterwards he was employed as tutor and chaplain in the household of Sir John Walsh, a prosperous Gloucestershire merchant. It is probable that there Tyndale was given much encouragement, both moral and financial.

In 1515 Tyndale was to be found in Cambridge where the famous scholar Desiderius Erasmus had recently been Professor of Divinity. Of Dutch birth his reputation was widespread and he liked to be known as 'a citizen of the world'. It is probable that Tyndale was greatly influenced by his Humanist outlook, the reliance on human intellect and capabilities rather than dependence on religion.

Erasmus was shocked by the state of the English Church at that time in which there were all too many abuses. It had been hard hit by the Black Death of 1348 in which one third of England's population was said to have perished. New priests had been appointed but many of these were of low character – idle, ignorant, often absentee and out for what they could get; but they had great powers over simple and gullible people, hearing confessions, absolving sins and extracting exorbitant taxes. Superstitions were encouraged, so too were pilgrimages (often barefoot) to shrines of saints with humble supplications. Of worse repute were some monasteries and nunneries into which young men and women took refuge in search of safe and easy lives. These might be paid for by local inhabitants in return for religious favours including large donations made by people on their deathbeds in the hope of gaining remission of purgatory (a place of temporary torment before qualifying for heaven). By these means some monasteries had become inordinately rich.

Outbreaks of discontent occurred, most notably in 1378 when there came a strong protest from an Oxford divine, John Wycliffe, who preached that clergy should forsake wealth and power and lead lives of poverty and holiness.

This was courageous as churchmen defended their privileges ferociously and heretics were burned at the stake. Wycliffe himself did not suffer this fate as he had the protection of a powerful nobleman, John of Gaunt, younger son of King Edward III. After his death in 1384 his movement died down for a time, but it was to be revived by followers known as Lollards, and Wycliffe was held in honour as 'The Morning Star of the Reformation'. In 1381 the so-called Peasants' Revolt was directed mainly against the Church which was seen as their principal persecutor.

Although the Roman Church was to remain supreme, ordering people's lives and faiths in every detail, there were signs that its powers were declining. Men were beginning to think for themselves more, and independent thought was greatly advanced by a crucial invention, that of the printing press – in Germany c.1439 by Johannes Gutenberg and brought to England in 1476 by William Caxton. With more books available to more people, education was no longer confined to the clergy.

While Tyndale was in Cambridge it was evident that a new wind was blowing. This came to a head in 1517 when a German friar and professor of theology, Martin Luther, made a much-publicised protest when he was said to have posted on the walls of Wittenberg Castle a thesis containing ninety-five reasons for the wrongfulness of the sale of indulgences. These were documents purporting to forgive not only past sins but also ones to be committed in the future, once described as a passport to heaven.

For too long religion in Europe had been a matter of myths and miracles with total subservience to the Roman Church. Now a new freedom was born, the essence of which was salvation by faith and the grace of God rather than by deeds such as pilgrimages, abasement before the effigies of saints and the purchase of indulgences. Salvation no longer needed the blessings of the Church; greater reliance was put on human conscience and rational intelligence; and in all doctrines the ultimate authority was the scriptures not the Pope.

Of this New Learning, as it was called, Erasmus was a leading light and so too was Tyndale to become. He heeded especially the words of Erasmus that Christ desires his mysteries to be spread abroad as widely as possible. He became obsessed with the idea of producing a new translation of the Bible in language readily intelligible to all kinds of people (known as the Vernacular). He told a priest: 'I will cause a boy that driveth a plough shall know more of the scriptures than thou dost.' Tyndale had an extraordinary gift for learning languages,[1] as well as unique literary powers. He determined not to rely too much on the Latin version of the Scriptures known as The Vulgate. He would return to the Greek and to the Hebrew, but here there were difficulties, as Hebrew was not readily accessible; it was not taught at Oxford and could only be picked up by grammars of a sort and various treatises. He was full of hope that he would be assisted in this task by senior members of the Church, but help was not forthcoming. The priesthood had little interest in a Bible in the Vernacular open to all, for it suited them to have an ignorant and submissive flock.

Failing to find support in England, Tyndale went abroad in 1524 at first to Germany where in Cologne, following the Lutheran agitation, there was sympathy for the New Learning and, perhaps more importantly, many up-to-date printing presses; but there he was not to be left in peace to start on his translation of the New Testament. The dominant power was that of the Holy Roman Emperor Charles V, a strong opponent of Lutheranism. It became necessary for Tyndale

---

1 In time he was to master eight languages – English, Latin, Greek, Hebrew, French, German, Spanish and Italian.

to be constantly on the move from one bolthole to another in danger and privation while he worked on his masterpiece which was to transform the English language.

England had at first been resistant to Luther. He had found no favour with Henry VIII who wrote an *Assertio* condemning 'the corrupt teachings of this weed, this dilapidated sick and evil minded sheep.' In return, Luther made a bitter attack on Henry, describing him as 'a sacrilegious brigand', 'more of a trivial buffoon than a king', and 'raving like a strumpet in a tantrum.' For his *Assertio*, Pope Leo V awarded Henry the title of *Fidei Defensor* (Defender of the Faith) borne by English sovereigns ever since. Henry's anti-Lutheranism was to intensify and he ordered his Lord Chancellor, Thomas Wolsey, to suppress the movement ruthlessly which he started to do in 1521 with a ceremonial bonfire of Luther's works outside Saint Paul's Cathedral. In the following year the first Lutheran heretic was burned at the stake. These conflagrations became more frequent when in 1529 Wolsey was succeeded as Lord Chancellor by Sir Thomas More.

In his youth More had been a highly renowned scholar of saintly reputation, a close friend and confidant of the king and author of a famous book, *Utopia*, portraying an ideal state with a perfect society. He was described by a contemporary as 'one of the glories of our age.' But there was another side to him. He came to regard Lutheranism as a major threat to the Catholic church which had to be eliminated ruthlessly, regardless of pity, mercy or compassion. 'I feel that breed of men absolutely loathsome', he declared, 'and I want to be as hateful to them as anyone could possibly be.' In this determination he became fanatical, convinced that to be saved from hell's fire heretics had to be burned alive in this world. 'This', More said, 'was lawful, necessary and well done.' He seemed to delight in his purpose, even setting up a torment chamber in his own garden. Seldom has England been under such a vicious tyranny and it is indeed ironical that it should have occurred with a man such as More at the helm.

More did not confine his witch hunt to England; he also hunted down heretics abroad and these included Tyndale whom he described as 'a hellhound in the kennel of the Devil', 'worse than Sodom and Gomorrah' and 'the most dangerous man in Tudor England', while Tyndale said that More was 'the most cruel enemy of truth.' He had had great hopes that his 1526 version of the New Testament would be received enthusiastically in England, and was appalled when it was described as 'venomous and pestiferous', banned and ceremonially burned. This shocked him profoundly; such treatment of the word of God was gross profanity. However, he then set about a wholesale revision of it, finding an estimated five thousand corrections and improvements. The revision was completed in 1534 and was to become Tyndale's standard version of the New Testament, later to become the mainstay of the King James Bible, otherwise The Authorised Version. It was important at the time as it disproved the belief of some that English was too crude a language for the scriptures. It also showed up differences of interpretations between the Old Learning and the New. Protestantism was given a boost and Tyndale became one of its leading lights.

Following publication, this version was swiftly recognised as something special, even unique – so beautifully written, lucid and lyrical. So many of its phrases ('Let there be light', 'Eat, drink and be merry', and 'Fight the good fight' to name but three) passed into common use that Tyndale claimed 'the noise of the New Bible echoed throughout the country.'

It was to echo more strongly still with a significant change in England. By 1527 Henry had been married to his first wife Catherine of Aragon for eighteen years. She was a devout and virtuous woman but had been unable to give birth to a male heir which Henry wanted desperately as without one there was the probability of England on his death relapsing once again into civil war. He had also become totally infatuated with Anne Boleyn, a lady of the court – no great beauty but intelligent with a sharp tongue, a fiery temperament and steely determination. She was also said to have sympathy with New Learning including translations of the Bible into English. Henry longed to marry her but could not do so until his marriage to Catherine was annulled by the Pope, and Wolsey was commissioned to bring this about. Pope Clement VII might have agreed to it, but at that time he was a prisoner of the Habsburg Emperor Charles V who was Catherine's nephew and was firmly opposed to his aunt being set aside in this way, and the Pope had to conform. An impasse was reached and Henry was to take the law into his own hands, making himself in 1531 sole Protector and Supreme Head of the English Church and Clergy. Relations between Henry and the Pope deteriorated when in 1533 Pope Clement, under pressure from the Emperor, finally declared that Henry's marriage to Catherine was legal and could not be annulled.

This brought about a hardening in Henry's attitude towards the Papacy and, to some extent a leaning towards Luther and Protestantism. He became increasingly determined to have his way. In that year he married Anne Boleyn despite his marriage to Catherine being still intact, thus becoming a bigamist. For seven years Anne had held him in thrall, but her marriage to him depended on her bearing him a son which she was unable to do.[2] In 1535 came the execution of Sir Thomas More, who as a devout Catholic could not accept Henry as Supreme Head of the Anglican Church. Destined to controversy, to some More is a malignant misguided sadist,

---

[2] She was executed three years later after giving birth to the future Queen Elizabeth.

to others a heroic moral character.³

After the death of More, Henry took on as his right-hand man one of a very different hue. Thomas Cromwell was the son of a Putney blacksmith-cum-brewer, rugged, ruthless and as tough as they come. Of no strong religious beliefs of his own, he was aware of the winds of change and set his sails accordingly. He inclined towards Protestantism and took a leading part in the break with Rome and Henry's marriage to Anne Boleyn; and it was he who was to enforce the closing of the monasteries. No one was more responsible than he for the Reformation in England. He had, however, always to watch the moods of his master. He saw that at heart Henry was still a Catholic and wanted to retain as much Catholicism as was consonant with the annulment of his marriage: the Bible was kept in Latin as was the Mass; confessions and contrition (voluntary self-punishment) also remained. Protestants had as much to fear from him as Catholics, and Cromwell was told to lure Tyndale to England with assurances of personal safety and an honourable standing. Busy with his translations, Tyndale remained in Belgium, though there were others who sought him out. As a leading light of Protestantism he was a main target of Charles V Holy Roman Emperor and the Pope; and Henry VIII had been greatly incensed when he stated publicly that there were no grounds for the annulment of his marriage to Catherine.

Still, Tyndale occupied himself with the translation of the Old Testament from Hebrew into English. This he did with his usual flair and facility, enlightening obscure passages and enlivening the text with attractive phraseology ('Let there be light', 'Fat of the land', 'Am I my brother's keeper', 'Bringing down my grey hairs with sorrow to the grave'), many of which passed into the English language for general use.

---

3   Some four hundred years later he was canonised as a saint.

Tyndale worked in hardship and ever-present danger, but he did not weaken. There were no thoughts of giving up; he never lost sight of the great purpose in his life; and it was evident that he had no notions of his own greatness. He was by nature a man of benevolence and humility. A companion said of him that he was 'a man of most virtuous disposition and of life unspotted, doing good deeds secretly and being content with conscience of well doing.' All he wanted was to be left in peace to get on with his work. Tragically, this was not to be.

The judicial murder of William Tyndale was one of the most dastardly acts in English history. It was mainly due to one man. Henry Phillips came from a well-to-do family. His father had been a member of parliament and sheriff for the county of Gloucestershire; and he himself was a Bachelor of Civil Law from Oxford. It seems that in his youth he had gambled recklessly and lost a fortune which he was desperate to retrieve. Thus he was capable of any treachery or deceit for money. It remains unknown who put him up to the job but a likely candidate is John Stokesley, Bishop of London, who had always been an ardent persecutor of heretics and took pride in the number he had sent to be burned.

In 1535 Tyndale was living in the house of Thomas Poyntz, a prosperous English merchant in Antwerp, a city in which there was much support for Protestantism. There he was reasonably secure and making progress with his translation of the Old Testament of which he had completed the first five books (known as The Pentateuch). Phillip's objective was to inveigle himself into Poyntz's household, ingratiate himself with Tyndale and entrap him. This he was able to do while Poyntz was away on a business trip, and he found Tyndale an easy victim. All too ready to see the best in people, Tyndale readily succumbed to Phillips' blandishments and was easily enticed into heretical indiscretions so that Phillips in conjunction with the procurer-general of the Emperor

Charles V contrived to have him arrested and imprisoned in the castle of Vilvorde, several miles outside Antwerp where he was to remain for a year and a half, visited from time to time by legal pundits, doctors of divinity and passing friars who tried to make him recant. This he would not do and he was brought to trial in October 1536. He was declared guilty of heresy and condemned to a horrific death – strangled first by the executioner and his corpse, perhaps with some life still in it, tossed on to a bonfire. His last words were: 'Lord, open the king of England's eyes.'

And so perished one of England's brightest lights. His achievements had been a marvel, and it was not long before his last prayer was soon answered in part. Protestantism was not to be stamped out; as has often been the case, the more a sect is persecuted the more it grows. In 1538 the breach with Rome was completed when Henry VIII was excommunicated by Pope Paul III.[4] In 1536 smaller monasteries had been closed down and so too in 1539 were the larger ones. In that year too it was ordained that a Bible in English should be placed in every parish.[5]

For a time it was not fully realised how great was the debt owed to Tyndale. There were others who stole his thunder. When in 1611 the King James Bible appeared it was assumed that it was the work of the fifty scholars, as well as the king himself, who had been at work on it for the last five years. It was only later when a careful examination was made that it was found to be overwhelmingly the Tyndale version. Later it was to be considered how profound had been the effects of the Authorised Version – that it had been a unifying force and had paved the way to a more egalitarian society.

---

4 Henry declaring that he 'didn't care a fig about the Pope's excommunication.'

5 Known as The Great Bible based largely on the version of Tyndale.

As the flames lapped around him in 1536 Tyndale might have been comforted by the words of Bishop Latimer twenty years later when he was in the same predicament – that he was 'lighting a candle by God's grace in England as shall never be put out.'

JEAN-JACQUES ROUSSEAU

(1712—1778)

Few would have predicted that Jean-Jacques Rousseau, ne'er-do-well son of a Swiss watchmaker, would become in time a political philosopher of universal influence. Maximilien Robespierre, the fanatical French revolutionary, was to say of him that he was 'the one man who through the loftiness of his soul and the grandeur of his character showed himself worthy of the role of teacher of mankind.' There were, however, those who took a different view. Voltaire, at the heart of the 18th century French Enlightenment, described him as 'a monster of vanity and violence.'

Rousseau was born in Geneva in 1712. His mother died when he was a baby, his elder brother of whom he was fond was to be sent away to a reformatory, and he himself was to be pampered by his father, of whom he had a low opinion, and who encouraged him in his belief that he was 'a prophet of truth and virtue and that he and only he had an inestimable gift to bestow on humanity and to become its saviour.'

The story of his early life was one of failure and frustration: in everything to which he put his hand – farmer, tutor, musician, among others – he was unsuccessful. For a time he was secretary to the French diplomat Comte de Montaigu who dismissed him, describing him as a man 'of vile disposition and unspeakable insolence, the product of his insanity and high opinion of himself.' He ended up as kept man of Madame de Warens, a royal pensioner, which was to last fourteen years; it is reported that never did he express any gratitude for this rescue from destitution, and made no move to come to her aid when she was impoverished and dying of starvation, a bitter humiliation for one who looked on himself as a great apostle of 'truth, liberty and virtue.'

When he was thirty-three he took up with Thérèse Levasseur, a laundress nine years younger than himself who was to stand by him for more than twenty years, acting partly as nanny and partly as mistress. He was to say of her that he never felt the least glimmer of love, treating her callously and dispassionately as a servant rather than as a hostess and that the sensual needs he satisfied with her were no more than physical. In turn, she said of him: 'I have been twenty-two years with Monsieur Rousseau and I would not give up my place to be Queen of France.'

Rousseau's early life showed he could be coarse, heartless and quarrelsome; far from a virtuous lover of humanity. His saving grace was as his gift as a writer, and this did not emerge until 1750 when he was thirty-eight. In that year he entered a competition for an essay on a theme 'Has the rebirth of science and the arts contributed to an improvement of morals?' In this he might have taken the popular view which would have been strongly in the affirmative, but he decided that it would be more conspicuous if he took a vigorous contrary view, which he did. Rousseau won the prize, gaining him great notoriety.

It was a time of change. The *Ancien Regime* had long been accustomed to tradition and convention, the long-established doctrines and authority of the church undisputed. But new ideas were intervening. Dissent and disillusionment were rife and it was de rigueur to argue and dispute. Rousseau quickly became aware that he would attract more attention as an angry irreverent voice than as a sycophant, so he became as rude and intemperate as he felt inclined – especially, it seemed, towards those who had shown him most favour.

Of all the events in his life which show Rousseau at his worst was the treatment meted out to the five children he fathered by Thérèse Levasseur. He insisted that these be put at once into an orphanage, the grim and terrible Hôpital des Enfants-trouvés.[1] The horror was made only worse by the hypocrisy that went with it. Rousseau declared the orphanage the best thing possible for them, that it made them more robust and that he only wished his upbringing had been the same. 'I know full well,' he declared, 'that no father is more tender than I would have been.' Certainly, he took no further interest in them.

In spite of his boorishness and offensiveness Rousseau was to become a cult figure. There were those who could not but be overwhelmed by his vivacity, mesmeric language and overweening belief in his own righteousness. To them he was bringing a new voice into a moribund society, enlivening existence, even making it worthwhile. Religion, he urged, should no longer be based on superstition, miracles and holy writ but on instinct and natural feeling. His great concept was that Man was born into the world free, innocent and undefiled, and was then corrupted by modern civilisation based on competitiveness and greed. 'Man is born free', he proclaimed grandiloquently, 'and is everywhere in chains.'

---

1   It was reckoned that of the three thousand or so of infants deposited there barely one third survived.

For his free speech, Voltaire had served a term in the Bastille and had been submitted to a public caning. Rousseau was to avoid such punishment but lived in constant danger.

At the age of forty in 1752, Rousseau embarked on the work for which he became best known, *The Social Contract*. Taking ten years to complete, its message was that a new society was to be formed, egalitarian but authoritarian. Men and women would give up the rights to control their lives in exchange for an equal part in settling general rules of the society. Private property was declared to be one of the main causes of evil, and this was to be kept to a minimum and as far as possible equally distributed. This new state would take charge of all children from birth and would inculcate virtue into them. Their thoughts and upbringing would be strictly controlled; it being realised that those who controlled opinions controlled actions. They would be indoctrinated into malleable and law-abiding citizens with social law planted in their hearts. As adults they would still be treated as children with the state as parent. The state would form the minds of all and there would be no individualism. Above all there would be total acceptance and obedience to the General Will, which was not dissimilar to Big Brother in George Orwell's *Nineteen Eighty-Four*. Who wielded the power behind General Will was not apparent.

In spite of the admiration that surrounded him Rousseau was seldom happy. He was beset by a persecution mania, verging on dementia, which made him feel that everyone was plotting against him. He also suffered chronic ill health (necessitating the use of a catheter), which shamed and embittered him. He was seldom at ease.

The wonder was that in spite of his uncouth and unpleasant ways he remained so popular. People were overawed by his flow of words, eloquent if not readily intelligible; his admirers included the elite and the erudite. Immanuel Kant, the German philosopher, wrote of 'his sensibility of soul of unequalled perfection'; and Friedrich Schiller, poet and dramatist, wrote of 'his Christlike soul for whom only heaven's angels are fit company.' And to the poet Percy Bysshe Shelley he was 'a sublime genius.' Not everyone, however, was enchanted. The philosopher Denis Diderot to whom he owed so much for his rise to fame, wrote of him as 'deceitful, vain as Satan, ungrateful, cruel, hypocritical and full of malice,' while David Hume, the Scottish philosopher who had once described him as 'gentle, modest, affectionate, disinterested, exquisitively sensitive', revised his opinion to a 'monster who saw himself as the only important thing in the universe.'

Rousseau knew how to play to the gallery with eccentric behaviour and bizarre clothing and hairstyles. He was also prepared to reveal intimate secrets of his life – what he called 'the dark and dirty labyrinth of his sex life.'[2] His *Confessions* were written in 1770 but not published until after his death in 1778.

To civilisation, Rousseau was a mixed blessing. To some he may have opened up new vistas, giving them a healthier, happier and more enlightened life, but the dictatorship he depicted in *The Social Contract* had fatal and far-reaching consequences. In it he made the error of assuming ideas were of supreme importance, that ideas were to be imposed forcefully on receptive human beings, rather than adapting these ideas to the ways of humanity. It was thought by many that *The Social Contract* sowed the seeds of the French Revolution and the Reign of Terror, and in later centuries paved the way for the mass murders of Hitler, Stalin and Mao Tse Tung. Such events would have appalled Rousseau who

---

2   These were indeed dark and dirty. They included baring his bottom to women who passed him in the street and being spanked by formidable females.

had once declared himself strongly opposed to revolution. 'Think of the dangers,' he once wrote, 'of setting the masses in motion. People who make revolutions nearly always end by handing themselves over to tempters who make their chains heavier than before. I would not have anything to do with revolutionary plots which always lead to disorder, violence and bloodshed.'[3] But there were to be thousands, even millions, who welcomed such events and looked on them as a deliverance into a new and better world.

Long after his death there were those who revered him and accepted his own self-valuation as the most virtuous man of his time. Pilgrims from all parts of the world came to his tomb to pay reverence to Rousseau.

---

3   Quoted from *Intellectuals* by Paul Johnson, Weidenfeld and Nicolson, 1988.

THOMAS PAINE

(1737—1809)

In the 18th century there was no more controversial figure than Thomas Paine. John Adams, second US President, said of him: 'I know not whether anyone in the world has had more influence on its inhabitants or affairs for the last thirty years than Tom Paine.' To Theodore Roosevelt, a later President, he was 'A dirty little atheist.'

Thomas Paine was born in 1737 in Thetford in Norfolk in humble circumstances. His father Joseph Paine (once Pain) was an artisan specialising in the making of stays for ladies' corsets; his mother Frances came from a higher order, daughter of a successful lawyer. At an early age Thomas was apprenticed into the trade of corset making, but the Fates had in store for him a more adventurous career than that of corsetier. His youth was unsettled: he was to be heard of at various times as shopkeeper, tutor and excise officer.[1] In none of these callings, however, did he make much of a mark, and

---

1   Collecting duties on such important articles as brandy, wine and tobacco. An unpopular office.

so in 1774 at the age of thirty-seven he set out to seek his fortune in the English colonies in America.

After a fearful and near fatal transatlantic crossing, he ended up in Philadelphia where at that time rebellion was in the air mainly concerning the right of the English government to tax the colonists without representation in the British parliament. There had been several hostile incidents including in the previous year the so-called Boston Tea Party.

Paine found himself a job with a newly established printshop and bookstore, the *Pennsylvania Magazine*, where he was found to have a fluent and cogent literary style. His first article was an attack on slavery, but in 1776 he published a pamphlet with the title *Common Sense* which was to have phenomenal success – circulation was said to have been as high as 500,000. In this he set out clearly and starkly the disadvantages of the colonies maintaining their links with Britain. In particular, he emphasised that they had no need of a monarch – remote and unsympathetic far away across the seas with little knowledge of American ways of life and always putting British interests first. And the history of the British monarchy was not impressive. There was nothing mystical about it. Kings and queens were descended from William the Conqueror, a none too reputable French chieftain of Norse descent, illegitimate and grandson of a tanner, who at the head of a mixed bag of adventurers had made himself king of England against the wishes of the native population. So much for the myth of Divine Right of Kings. And since the Norman Conquest the record of most monarchs had been warlike and despotic. There had been thirty kings and two minors, and during their reigns there had been eight civil wars and nineteen rebellions. Hardly a peace-giving force. Was there not everything to be said for a republic, free of feudal privileges, peacefully inclined and locally elected? Was it not time for Americans to look after their own interests and map out their own future in the great continent into which they were expanding?

Paine's influence was so great that after the Declaration of Independence he was appointed secretary of the Committee of Foreign Affairs in Congress. Here, however, he showed himself to be irresponsible and had to be dismissed. For the remainder of the war he fought with the colonists, acting as aide-de-camp to General Nathanael Greene with the rank of brigadier; and when their fortunes were at their worst he issued a stirring address worthy of King Henry V at Agincourt:

> *These are the times that try men's souls: the summer soldier and the sunshine patriot will in this crisis shrink from the service of his country, but he that stands it now deserves the love and thanks of man and woman. Tyranny like hell is not easily conquered; yet we have this consolation with us, that the harder the conflict the more glorious the triumph. What we obtain too cheap we esteem too lightly. Tis dearness only that gives everything its value.*

Paine's return to England in 1787 (at the age of fifty) was mainly concerned with the building of an iron bridge he had designed. This was to prove unsuccessful, but in 1789 the French Revolution broke out. King Louis XVI had been compelled to assemble a parliament (States General), the first for 175 years; the grim prison fortress of the Bastille had been razed to the ground[2]; and a ragged crowd of fishwives, market women, prostitutes and disreputable vagabonds had set out on the twelve-mile trek to Versailles to fetch the royal family back to Paris; this they succeeded in doing, after nearly killing Queen Marie Antoinette, to the shouts of 'The baker, the

---

2   Found to contain no more than seven prisoners.

baker's wife', and preceded by the severed heads of murdered guardsmen stuck on spikes. It had become evident that there was nothing so dangerous as an angry ravenous mob.

In England the Revolution had found at first a mixed reception. There were those who welcomed it. The poet Wordsworth wrote:

Bliss it was at that dawn to be alive;
But to be young was very heaven.

There were others too who thought that revolution in France was overdue, and they rejoiced in the words of Richard Price, a Unitarian clergyman, that 'Thirty millions of people were demanding liberty with irresistible force and a despotic king was being led in triumph.' But as the Revolution gained in momentum and horror strong opposition was aroused, and the main spokesman of this was not a Tory aristocrat or royal prince but a Whig politician of Irish origins. Until then Edmund Burke had been a supporter of advanced and humanitarian causes. Of great erudition and eloquence, he had spoken out forcefully on such issues as the slave trade, the despotic depredations of the East India Company in India, and the rights of the American colonists. But the revolution in France filled him with fear, originating perhaps when in 1780 London was overrun by a hysterical mob led by a demented nobleman, Lord George Gordon, rioting in protest at a bill for the relief of Roman Catholics.[3]

Burke had besides a strong distrust of political theory. He had no time for schemes that proved by infallible logic how happy man would be if only his affairs were organised on an entirely new pattern. Man is not a logical animal, he

---

3   The Gordon Riots, as they were called, were graphically described in Dickens's novel *Barnaby Rudge*.

maintained. The present social and political system (rotten boroughs and all[4]) was a product of past experience. It worked – something to be glorified not despised. Hold fast to everything, then. Alter nothing. Better to endure those ills than to fly to others we know not of. Hereditary succession was attended with fewer evils than frequent elections. These would result in the total subversion of the established form of government. Wise beneficent aristocrats would be replaced by 'petty lawyers, constables, Jew-brokers, keepers of hotels, taverns, brothels, shop boys, hairdressers, fiddlers and dancers, snatched from the humblest ranks of subordinates.' To these views he gave full vent in a pamphlet he published in 1790, titled *Reflections on Revolution in France*. This was received with wide approbation and was one of the causes of British governments for the next forty-seven years being rigidly opposed to any form of change.

Such views were of course anathema to Paine and in 1791 he published *The Rights of Man*, the first of two pamphlets. In this against Burke's praise of tradition, property and heredity he put equality, freedom and reason. He asserted that government derived from the people and could be altered at their will and had to be carried on for their benefit through popular representation; it was the inherent and inalienable right of people to rebel against a government if it did not safeguard their natural rights, and they were brought to destitution by arbitrary rule, poverty, illiteracy, unemployment or war. Although comparatively mild in tone, *The Rights of Man*, like *Common Sense* made a great impact. There was something about Paine's writing which made people sit up and take notice. Along with the French Revolution it awakened political awareness in a new class of

---

4   Whereby a derelict site like Old Sarum returned two members of parliament while the growing city of Manchester returned none.

'Wha Wants Me', cartoon showing Tom Paine and
the Rights of Man by Isaac Cruikshank (1756-1811/16) /
British Library, London, UK

© British Library Board. All Rights Reserved / Bridgeman Images

people. Artisans, shopkeepers, clerks and small businessmen became disinclined to leave politics to royalty and aristocracy. Working men's political clubs and so-called Corresponding Societies were set up and eagerly attended especially by those newly literate. Debates in these became ever more lively when in 1792 a Second Part to *Rights of Man* was published.

This was more vituperative and inflammatory. It demanded the end of all hereditary rights including the monarchy,[5] the House of Lords and privileges of the clergy with separation of church and state. It urged that the dominion of kings be replaced by that of laws and the dominion of priests by reason and conscience. Governments of course should be chosen not by heredity but by the votes of common people. It also called for free education for the poor, with pensions and maternity benefits to be paid for by a graduated income tax.

Although the government of the Younger Pitt had been agitated by the first part of *The Rights of Man*, nothing could be found in it that was indictable; though the Home Secretary Henry Dundas saw to it that Paine's life was made dangerous and disagreeable by the activities of the political police, and that copies of the pamphlet were difficult, indeed illegal, to obtain. With the publication of the Second Part, Dundas felt that action was necessary, and a warrant was issued for Paine's arrest on a charge of seditious libel. However, he was warned of his danger just in time for him to escape to France.

In his polemical confrontation with Burke the latter had seemed to prevail; the French Revolution did end in widespread bloodshed and tyranny and military dictatorship leading to a prolonged European war, whereas the views of Paine were strongly condemned. But with the passing of time a different story was to be told with the coming of the welfare state.

---

5   The unfortunate George III had just been found mad, and Paine had written of him cruelly as His Mad-jesty.

Tom Paine's escape from England was accompanied by jeers and clenched fists, but he was greeted in France with enthusiasm. His part in the American Revolution was recognised and he was made an honorary French citizen and elected to the National Convention, as the French parliament was then called. There a bitter struggle was taking place between two main parties – the moderate Girondists and extremists known as Jacobins. Gradually the latter were gaining the upper hand, and increasingly so after the fiasco of the king and queen's attempted escape out of the country. This was to settle their fate. Soon afterwards the king was put on trial of which Paine was in favour, and then condemned to death which he opposed, stating forebodingly that 'he who would make his own liberty secure must guard even his own enemy from repression, for if he violates this duty he establishes a precedent that will reach to himself.'

The power of the Jacobins increased further when one of their leaders, Jean Paul Marat, was assassinated – in his bath with a carving knife by Charlotte Corday, an idealistic young woman from Normandy who hoped this would be a death blow to the Jacobins, but the opposite proved to be the case. Marat was hailed as a martyr and Jacobins became more extreme. Louis XVI was guillotined in horrific circumstances as was Queen Marie Antoinette soon afterwards.[6] The Younger Pitt, the prime minister of England, described their execution as 'the foulest and most atrocious deed which the history of the world had as yet had occasion to attest.' It caused shock and horror throughout Europe and was one of the reasons why several countries were to declare war on France. Nevertheless, the power of the Jacobins continued to increase, and by 1793 the Girondins had been virtually eliminated, and a reign of

---

6   The guillotine was a contraption recently introduced for cutting off heads. Its inventor described it as 'prompt and expeditious.'

terror spread across the country. Life became frighteningly cheap. In revolutionary fervour, it was not safe even to sit on the sidelines. It was blazoned abroad that those who make revolution by halves dig their own graves. Having disposed of the king and queen and all aristocrats they could find, revolutionary leaders then turned on themselves. In 1794 Georges Danton, one of the most potent of revolutionary leaders, was sent to the guillotine for supposed moderation, leaving as virtual dictator Maximilien Robespierre whose solution to every problem was the guillotine. But then he too was brought down and put to death along with one hundred and eight of his followers.

Paine had escaped death by a hairbreadth. A target ever since opposing the execution of the king, he had not escaped imprisonment. He was arrested soon after Christmas Day in 1793 and swept off to the horrors of the Luxembourg, once a luxurious palace, then a ghastly prison. It was expected that as an American citizen he might soon be released but this was not to happen (mainly, it seems, because of the personal antipathy of the American minister in Paris, one Gouvernour Morris, and George Washington in America taking no action on his behalf). He was imprisoned in vile conditions for ten months and nine days, of which for six months he had no contact at all with the outside world. Each day saw an exodus of twenty or thirty prisoners on their way to the guillotine. Those remaining must have spent each day wondering if it was to be their last.

Sensing his days were numbered, before his imprisonment Paine had engaged on another major work. His religion had been mixed. His father had been a Quaker and his mother a member of the Church of England. Later he had had Methodist leanings but soon became a free thinker and was much influenced by a form of Deism. The essence of this was belief in one God, creator of the universe but who keeps apart from it and does not intervene in human life and leaves his creation to look after itself as best it can by means of natural laws. Human beings then are free agents in a free world to go their own way with the right to their own religions and to practice these when, where and with whom they pleased. This meant that Paine became strongly opposed to organised religions. He thought them despotic and deceptive, riddled with superstition and fanaticism, leading to unequal wealth, power-hungry priests and the enslavement of mankind. The Old Testament he wrote off as a history of corruption, cruelty and evil ways with no revelation of the word of God. He had respect for the moral teachings of Christ in the New Testament but no belief in his divinity nor his miracles; and he considered the Gospel generally to be inconsistent and often misleading and too much influenced by Judaism. He retained, however, a belief in a God who was a benevolent creator of a marvellous universe by whose laws all should be guided.

With these beliefs he was greatly disturbed by the actions of the Jacobins who were compelling all to become atheists and were actively engaged in 'dechristianising' the country – closing churches, destroying religious books, desecrating religious paintings, demolishing church towers; even deconsecrating the great cathedral of Notre Dame and renaming it A Temple of Reason.

Tom Paine came out of prison on 6 November 1794 plagued by gout, recurrent fever and mental instability. He was taken into the household of James Monroe who had replaced Gouvernour Morris as ambassador to France and who recognised the great debt owed to Paine by the American people. He was to stay with him for eighteen months and then for five years with his publisher Nicolas de Bonneville. It had not been possible for him to return to America; with France and England at war the Atlantic crossing was simply too dangerous. If he was captured by an English man-of-war and taken back to England a death sentence would have been certain. In Paris he was treated as a hero by some but with abhorrence as a malignant atheist by others. He was to become associated for a time with Napoleon Bonaparte and they plotted together an invasion of England; but they soon parted company. Napoleon had a great admiration for Paine and was quoted as saying that a statue of gold should be erected to him in every city on the universe. But this admiration was not reciprocated, Paine describing Napoleon as 'the completest charlatan that ever existed on the face of the earth – wilful, headstrong, proud, morose, presumptuous.'

During these years Paine also made an embittered attack on George Washington, prompted by his conviction that he had done nothing to have him released from prison and wanted him to die there. He described his one-time friend as a weak and hesitant commander-in-chief, dependent entirely on assistance from France. This opinion, however, was contradicted by most people including Frederick the Great, king of Prussia, who asserted that one of Washington's campaigns was 'the most brilliant of any recorded in the history of military achievements.'

Paine had faced up to the failure of the French Revolution in which he had once gloried. Its early high ideals had been defamed and it had descended into an orgy of bloodshed and abuse. In 1793 he had written to Thomas Jefferson: 'Had the Revolution been conducted consistent with its principles there was once a good prospect of extending liberty through the greatest parts of Europe, but now I relinquish that hope.' Later he was to say plaintively: 'They have conquered all Europe only to make it more miserable than it was before.' The general atmosphere in America too had become one of despondency and disenchantment. George Washington had lost faith in democracy which had not brought in the golden age he had envisaged. New people were coming to the fore apparently interested only in making money and getting ahead. Others of the Founding Fathers were equally depressed. Alexander Hamilton had declared: 'This American world was not made for me.' And Thomas Jefferson, the main author of the Declaration of Independence, was to write: 'All, all are dead and ourselves left amid a new generation whom we know not and who knows not us.' Had Edmund Burke been right 'to put one's trust in hereditary rights and privileges?' Dreams of great Enlightenment had come to nought.

In 1802 the Treaty of Amiens brought a temporary break in the Anglo–French war which made it possible for Paine to return to America.

His arrival caused great agitation. There was a sharp division of opinion, some regarding him as a great hero of American Independence, others unable to forgive him for his denunciation of Christianity.

At that time there was bitter political rivalry between the so-called Federalists led by John Adams who had followed in the wake of George Washington with conservative leanings regarding government and foreign relations, favouring English customs and conventions, and the Democratic Party led by Thomas Jefferson more liberally inclined and closer to France. Jefferson had been elected President in 1800, and Paine had hopes he might be found a place in his administration, but this Jefferson regarded as dangerous. Paine was too controversial a character, not only because of his anti-Christian beliefs and his denunciation of Washington but also because of his physical condition. He had never fully recovered from his imprisonment; he still suffered agonies from gout and had deep depressions which brought on heavy drinking resulting in what was politely described as an inclination towards inebriety. Because of his dishevelled appearance and unwholesome habits he was kept at a distance by elite society.

He continued with his writing but this lacked the cogency it had once had. It brought him in money, but this he was unwilling to spend, leading rather a life of parsimony and indigence; and he was to incur stronger unpopularity. The first main biography of him by a New York newspaper editor, James Cheetham, was vicious and scurrilous, making him out as malignant and mendacious.

He died on 8 June 1809 at the age of 72. At his request he was buried in a lonely spot in farmland in Upstate New York. There were six people at his funeral. One obituary read: 'He had an excellent pen to write with but an indifferent head to think.' Another: 'He lived long – did some good and much bad.'

Yet his achievements had been phenomenal. He had had a crucial role in American independence, John Adams writing of him that 'without his pen the sword of Washington would have been drawn in vain.' He is also believed to have been the originator of the appellation United States of America. He had had a part too in the setting up of the Second French Republic. In addition, he had had three best-selling worldwide publications. And there was something further. In the second part of *The Rights of Man* as well as advocating the abolition of hereditary privileges and a government chosen by common people he had called for the introduction of such measures as old age pensions, maternity benefits and free education and medical care. At the time these were disregarded; they were too *avant garde*; but within 150 years they were to be enshrined in the political systems of most countries in the world.

No mean achievements for the corset maker from Thetford.

CHARLES DARWIN

(1809—1882)

ORIGIN OF SPECIES BY NATURAL SELECTION

Although Charles Darwin had no formal qualifications in science and was a shy and retiring man, he was, nevertheless, to make history.

He came from a well-to-do family in Shrewsbury where his father Robert was a rich and highly respected doctor.[1] At the age of ten Darwin went to Shrewsbury School where he was taught nothing much more than Latin and Greek which made little impression on him, and he was an undistinguished pupil. He was destined by his father for medicine and was sent to Edinburgh University to study for this, but it did not take him long to realise that medicine was not for him.[2] In

---

1   He was also one of the largest men in the country, weighing some twenty-four stone.

2   He was said to have been put off when he attended an operation on a child with no anaesthetic.

that case, what was? Not the army, the navy or the stage, leaving the Church as the only possibility. This too was a doubtful proposition. He was not particularly devotional and had little interest in theology; but this did not matter. The life of a country parson at that time was undemanding, leaving plenty of opportunity for other pursuits, which in Darwin's case proved to be natural history.

In 1830, at the age of twenty-one, he began his clerical studies at Cambridge University where he caught the eye of a distinguished scientist, the Rev. John Henslow, Professor of Botany. He invited Darwin to join a ship of the Royal Navy, H.M.S. *Beagle*, about to make a voyage of exploration on the coast of South America. Darwin would travel in the capacity of 'gentleman companion' to the captain, who on a long and lonesome voyage needed an associate from outside the Royal Navy with whom he could converse. The conditions on board would be rigorous and unpaid, but the post would afford him freedom for independent activity and great opportunities. Darwin was eager to accept the offer, but it depended on his father, who would bear the cost and at first was strongly opposed, regarding the trip as an irrelevant distraction, quite unsuitable for an intending clergyman. He would give his consent only if the project was strongly recommended by someone whose judgement he respected, and this was to be found in his brother-in-law Josiah Wedgwood of the famous pottery empire. And so Robert relented, promising 'all assistance in my power.'

There was much that was exciting about the impending voyage of H.M.S. *Beagle*. South America was largely unexplored and seemed to offer excellent openings for trade – lucrative markets for manufactured goods and a plentiful source of raw materials. The captain of the *Beagle*, Robert Fitzroy, was clearly a high flyer, captain of a man-of-war at the age of twenty-three and a well-informed scientist. He was also said to be descended from King Charles II by one of his mistresses, the nephew of a duke and the son of a general. He and Darwin seemed well matched which was as well, as living at close quarters on a long sea voyage would put a strain on their relationship, and there were to be times when this nearly broke down. In his autobiography Darwin was to write that as well as brilliant gifts, Fitzroy was also 'of uncertain temper and not easy to live with', but somehow they managed to keep together for nearly five years.

The first months of the voyage were inauspicious. Three times the departure dates had to be postponed because of faults in the ship or unfavourable winds and tides. This was especially unfortunate as at that time the great Reform Bill was being passed and England was in a state bordering on revolution. It was not until December 1831 that the *Beagle* was able to set sail, and then not too happily. The long delays had caused drunkenness and indiscipline on the lower deck, and Fitzroy had dealt with these in the time-honoured way of the Royal Navy – with the lash, some a hundred and thirty strokes being administered, the wails of the offenders mingling with the sounds of gales which in the Bay of Biscay were fierce, causing Darwin to be painfully seasick. And then when the ship reached the Canary Islands it was put in quarantine because of an outbreak of cholera in England, and no landings were allowed. These were not to occur until the *Beagle* reached Cape Verde Islands, a mass of desolate volcanic hills. It was not before 28 February, 1832 that the ship finally reached the mainland of Brazil in Bahia in San Salvador and Darwin was able to set about those things he had come out to do – examining rock formations, looking for fossils of extinct animals and collecting specimens of rare plants and animals (to be sent back to England), visiting tropical forests and coral islands. In April 1832 the *Beagle* was in Rio de Janeiro and three months later in Montevideo and

Buenos Aires. In 1833 the ship visited the Falkland Islands (then known as Malvinas) and Tierra del Fuego where Darwin came across primitive people existing in caves and dugouts, covered only in animal skins. In 1834, after repairs to the *Beagle* in Buenos Aires, the vessel was ready to go round Cape Horn into the Pacific into which it sailed in May (two and a half years after leaving England) and in July the company had reached Valparaiso in Chile, a comparatively civilised place where further repairs to the *Beagle* could be undertaken and stores replenished. Shortly after leaving, the ship found itself in the midst of an earthquake which was terrifying, but it survived and in September 1835 arrived in the Galapagos Islands where there were no rock formations of interest but a unique variety of animals including giant tortoises which could live for over a hundred years.

The visit to Galapagos was perhaps the climax of the voyage as far as Darwin was concerned. It was there he could no longer blind himself to a conviction on which he had long been ruminating.

At the end of the 18th century a group of scientists had been promulgating the belief that the Biblical account of the Creation was impossible. This laid it down that at a certain time God had created the universe in seven days and had then created animals to inhabit it, and these included Man made in his own image: a theologian had estimated that this had taken place some six thousand years ago; and this had been generally accepted. However, geologists had been excavating deep into the earth examining rock formations and discovering ancient fossils of extinct animals; and their conclusions were definite: the Earth had been in existence for millions of years and there had been life there, including human life, far into antiquity. They also found that there had been no sudden creation but the world had been permanently in a state of change and growth, and if this was true of the

Charles Darwin on the Galapagos Islands, Howat,
Andrew (20th Century) / Private Collection
© Look and Learn / Bridgeman Images

Earth it was also true of animals; they too had not been individually created but had developed out of other species and were still in a state of evolution, changing according to their environments and circumstances of life. Thus animals in cold climates had developed warm coats, those on great plains or open spaces developed powerful muscles for running, and those who lived in trees developed hands which could grip, and camels developed humps.

Darwin was acquainted with these theories but had not much heeded them. However, in the course of his voyage on the *Beagle* he could not but become aware of the enormous variety of plant and animal life. This was so great that it seemed impossible that all could have been created separately. The evidence was mounting that all species had originated from the same source and had evolved into a multiplicity of differences.

These theories brought great distress to Darwin. He realised what they entailed. The stories in the Book of Genesis – of the Garden of Eden, the Tower of Babel and Noah's Ark were no more than allegorical fables, not a revelation of God. More seriously, the Christian religion was being undermined and the moral principles on which society was based threatened. Life was an unremitting struggle ('red in tooth and claw') for existence with the survival of the fittest and the elimination of the weakest. To Darwin this was anathema. 'Like confessing a murder' as he put it and 'living in hell.' Carried to their logical conclusion it was difficult to deny that Man had a common ancestry with anthropoid apes.

The *Beagle* left Galapagos in October 1835 and a month later had reached the hospitable and hedonistic French island of Tahiti; then on to New Zealand and Australia (January 1836), Mauritius (April 1836), South Africa round the Cape of Good Hope, across the Atlantic to San Salvador (August 1836) so that Captain Fitzroy could regulate his chronometers;

and at last in England, reaching Falmouth on 2 October 1836 after a voyage of four years and nine months (instead of the two years originally planned). During this time Darwin had spent long periods ashore – in geologising, collecting fossils and animal and plant specimens – travelling perhaps as many as two thousand miles on horseback. It had been an experience like no other but at the end of it Darwin declared: 'I abhor the sea and all ships that sail on it...The sea is no more than a tedious waste of water.'

On arrival back in England Darwin found himself immersed in activity. His family was anxious to meet him and find out how much he had changed and he himself wanted the latest developments with them, to discover that his sister Caroline had married their first cousin Jos Wedgwood and his youthful sweetheart Fanny Owen had become Mrs Myddleton-Biddulph with three children, leaving him somewhat out on a limb, and giving him serious thought to marriage which, he held, had not to interfere with his work; but in 1839 at the age of thirty he married his cousin Emma Wedgwood who was to prove a faithful and loving partner and, though uninterested in science and a devout Christian, was to stand by him for 43 years in all exigencies and to bear him ten children.

But it was not only among his family that Charles was in demand. While he had been away his patron, The Rev. John Henslow, Professor of Botany at Cambridge, had taken great care of all the fossils, species and memos he had sent back to him while away, and had seen to it that they fell into the right hands so that he had become a celebrity in scientific circles, although he still had no official standing. This, however, was rectified when in 1839 he was elected to the Royal Society.[3]

---

[3] The most prestigious scientific body in England if not the world, dating from the reign of Charles II and restricted in numbers, it was dedicated to the advancement of science.

In 1839 he published an adaptation of the diary he had kept during the voyage called *Journal of Researches into Geology and Natural History of Various Countries visited by HMS Beagle*. But this was only a preliminary to a full-scale work on *Origin of Species by Natural Selection* which he began writing in earnest in 1856, spurred on by the efforts of other scientists on the subject of evolution. If his work was to have the impact he wanted he would have to publish first. Otherwise his work would be regarded as secondary and himself guilty of plagiarism. Sorting and evaluating the thousands of species, memos and diary entries he had kept was hard laborious work, made worse by painful and debilitating bad health.

Darwin originally intended that The Big Species Book, as he sometimes called it, should be no longer than thirty or forty pages, but it was to expand to four hundred. It was to take him fifteen months and its publication in 1859 caused a sensation. Until then most people had not paid much heed to evolution, which was generally regarded as a quaint notion to be ignored or dabbled in lightly. But now people had to sit up and take notice; and they did not like what they found. Was it remotely possible that human beings were descended from monkeys? Darwin never said specifically that they were, only from 'a hairy quadruped furnished with a tail and pointed ears, probably arboreal in habits.' But that was enough to cause fury. Such a thing was not to be considered, and if it could not be refuted scientifically it was to be heaped with ridicule and abuse. 'The vilest and beastliest paradox ever invented,' said one. Another wrote: 'As for the idea that men are descended from monkeys, only monkeys would have allowed such an idea to enter their heads.' Others referred contemptuously to the 'monkey theory' and 'ourang-outang theology.' Not all, however, worked themselves into a frenzy. Benjamin Disraeli, one-time prime minister, could not take the matter too seriously, declaring light-heartedly that 'it seemed to be the case that man was either an ape or an angel in which case I am wholeheartedly on the side of the angels.'

In the debate that raged there were those who, while accepting the idea of evolution, could not bring themselves to break with the beauty and wisdom of their religion. How could it be possible, they wondered, that such a marvellous creation as that of the Universe could come about as a result of aimless natural forces? Surely it was the work of an almighty hand – a divine creation? There was also a body of opinion which accepted that evolution was possible among plants and animals, but not among mankind. This was unthinkable. There could be no connecting link between Man and other animals. Privately Darwin believed that there was, but this he kept to himself. 'I think,' he wrote, 'I shall avoid the whole subject, as so surrounded by prejudices, but I fully admit that it is the highest and most interesting problem for a naturalist.'

He determined, as far as possible, to leave it to others to fight his battles in public. One who was ready to do this was Thomas Huxley, a brilliant young biologist, who had been fired by *Origin of Species*, describing Darwin as 'the greatest revolutionist in natural history this century.' He wrote to Darwin: 'I am sharpening up my claws and beak in readiness.' And this he did with such acuity and forcefulness that he became known as 'Darwin's bulldog.'

A notable confrontation occurred between Huxley and Samuel Wilberforce, Bishop of Oxford (son of William Wilberforce, the great anti-slavery campaigner) when seven hundred people crammed into an Oxford library to hear them clash and listen to their arguments. In these Huxley was to have the upper hand after Wilberforce, usually suave and authoritative, made the mistake of taunting him as to whether it was from his grandfather or grandmother he was descended from an ape. This was thought to be bad taste in a serious discussion, and Huxley replied effectively that it was better to accept that monkeys were among one's forebears than to cover up the truth.

Among those present was Darwin's old shipmate Robert Fitzroy. Darwin always allowed that there were few to whom he owed so much. The voyage of HMS *Beagle* was the high point of his life and this would not have been possible without Fitzroy. His comradeship and helpfulness altered the course of his career. They had seen little of each other since the return of the *Beagle* twenty-four years before. Since then Darwin had grown to be of worldwide reputation while Fitzroy had suffered a series of misfortunes in both his public and personal life. He also felt himself tortured by the dispute between Scripture and Science and Evolution. As a devout Christian he held fast to the biblical traditions, but as a knowledgeable scientist he knew how vulnerable these were. In the end, the strain was too much for him and he took his own life.

Darwin himself was not present in Oxford. His health was bad and he was taking a water cure (hydrotherapy) in Yorkshire. Anyway, he preferred to be on the sidelines rather than the forefront of the battle. Honours and a glittering social life did not attract him. Truth rather than fame was what he sought. He preferred to live quietly and modestly in a Kentish backwater (Down House) with his wife and family, investigating those things that interested him – maybe climbing plants, orchids, worms. Although frequently impeded by bad health, he continued to publish, and even those on such abstruse subjects as the sexual colour of butterflies, *The Effects of Cross and Self-Fertilisation in the Vegetable Kingdom* and *Rats and Water Casks* were bestsellers so that he became a very rich man.

His death in 1882 at the age of seventy-three caused a stir worldwide. His reputation was then at its height. He had expected to be buried in the village churchyard of Down, but there was a general insistence that he should be buried in Westminster Abbey, this in spite of the fact that he had disavowed Christianity. After his death interest in evolution declined somewhat. Most Christians no longer took the book of *Genesis* literally. They might accept that Man had developed from a different sort of creature but this did not necessarily conflict with the existence of a Christian God. Most scientists too would not claim that evolution and natural selection could provide all the answers to the mysteries of life. One crucial question unanswered is the first appearance on earth of the first human being and the existence of a 'missing link' between mankind and animals. As the distinguished historian G. M. Trevelyan has put it: 'The whole truth about the universe cannot be discovered in a laboratory or divined by the Church.'

KARL MARX

(1818–1883)

'RELIGION IS THE OPIUM OF THE PEOPLE.'

Eighteen forty-eight A.D. was to become known as 'The Year of Revolutions.' These broke out all over Europe – in France, Germany, Italy and the Austrian Empire, and there came close to one in England where for a time a rebellious group known as Chartists posed a serious threat. Ultimately all of these came to nothing, but there occurred one event of long-term significance, the publication of *The Communist Manifesto*. This was primarily the work of a German–Jewish academic, Karl Marx.

Few people in future years were to have such widespread influence as Karl Marx. His doctrines spread all over the world and people high and low were to be affected by them. This was not due to military might. Marx was no great conqueror, 'wading through slaughter to a throne,'[1] but a professorial

---

1   From 'Elegy in a Country Churchyard' by Thomas Gray.

figure at a desk in a London public library, devouring printed matter, compiling statistics and writing a book which was to shake the world.

Marx was the son of a middle-class lawyer with deep roots in Judaism; among his forebears were many rabbis and Talmudic scholars. He had been educated at Bonn and Berlin universities where his main interests lay in philosophy and poetry. He was a distinguished scholar but not good enough for an academic career. He was to start life as a journalist and in Paris, where he became involved in revolutionary movements, he was expelled from the country, as he was from Belgium also before settling for thirty-four years in London where he had the reputation of an aggressive left-wing activist with a taste for strong language and violence. He was to spend most of his time in the Reading Room of the British Museum in what he called scientific political research; but this was hardly an apt description. If it had been he would have collected data of all sorts, collated them and drawn conclusions from them, instead of which he sought only such matter which supported his preconceived tendentious ideas – class warfare and seismic revolution. In the words of Paul Johnson, 'he was not interested in discovering truth but in proclaiming it.'[2]

He had persuaded himself that a great cataclysmic disaster was imminent in which society would collapse, culminating in the dictatorship of the proletariat, and this obsessed him. The main contention of *The Communist Manifesto* was that capitalism would be replaced by socialism and society would be reconstructed. It called for the abolition of inheritance tax and private property and a classless society. The long convoluted tracts on political economy, like many another, would probably not have seen the light of day but for some

---

2   *Intellectuals* (Weidenfeld and Nicolson, 1988).

ringing declarations which caught the public eye and became watchwords of revolution.[3]

In all Marx's writings, concerned as they mainly were with the triumph of the proletariat, there is hardly any mention of working men and women. With no interest in apocalyptic revolution but rather in gradual progressive improvements, Marx had as little contact with them as possible. To him doctrine was everything, practical reality invalid. For elections he had contempt, describing those in England as 'drunken orgies.' In the comfort and security of the British Museum, 'Far from the madding crowd's ignoble strife',[4] he could conjure visions of impending upsets with surging angry mobs, corpses hanging from lamp posts and guillotines in full swing, but he was never in the midst of them. To his fellow middle-class theoreticians, he would orate bombastically, so certain of his convictions that when contradicted he would roar furiously and scream abuse.

For most of Marx's life he was deskbound; he never set foot in factory, mine or dockyard. Such knowledge as he had of working-class conditions came from his friend and close colleague Friedrich Engels, who came from a well-to-do family in the Rhineland and who on a visit to Manchester had been so shocked by the lives of the cotton workers that he had written of them in a book entitled *Conditions of the Working Class in England*. This was an angry and bitter book, denouncing the British middle classes as callous and obdurate as they went on their daily round with 'mass murder, wholesale

---

3 As for example: 'workers have nothing to lose but their chains.' 'From each according to his abilities. To each according to his needs.' 'Religion is the opium of the people.' And there was a resounding call for working men in all countries to unite. Not all of these were original; some were borrowed from other sources, but they had great effect.

4 Thomas Gray, 'Elegy Written in a Country Churchyard'.

robbery and all the other crimes in the calendar.' He was to become Marx's chief political accomplice, collaborating closely with drawing up *The Communist Manifesto* and later *Das Kapital*, faithfully recording his master's every thought and ghosting many of his scripts. He also became manager of Marx's personal finances, which were always in confusion. He was to bring to these some measure of order as well as subsidising Marx when he was near to penury.

Although with a long line of rabbis and Talmudic scholars in his ancestry, Marx was not a religious man. For a time in his youth he had been of Christian faith but he had a strong aversion to organised religions, particularly Judaism – a religion, he said, in which money was God. For a time in his youth he had been a Lutheran Christian, but this had lapsed, and for most of his life he was atheist with a total lack of interest in Jewish affairs and a strong dislike of usury and banking which, he said, was 'a curse to the people.' He was also not to be drawn back to the tenets of Christianity. In later life he showed little sign of loving his neighbour as he himself and had little sympathy for the meek and the merciful; and if smitten on the right cheek he was unlikely to have turned the left.

The first part of *Das Kapital* was published in 1867 and was spread far and wide with aspiring intellectuals poring over its scripts in search of truth. As in *The Communist Manifesto*, Marx included only those facts and quotations in accordance with his essential beliefs, and some of these were thought to be so blatantly inaccurate that they gave rise to the suspicion that they were deliberate distortions or fabrications. As with *The Communist Manifesto*, *Das Kapital* was to have little immediate effect, but in time it was to become holy writ for dictators and mass murderers like Stalin in Russia and Mao Tse-Tung in China.

Marx's home life was a sad story of disorder and disharmony. Because of his immersion in dialectics, ordinary human habits like eating and washing tended to be neglected. As a result of an unhealthy diet (heavy drinking, strongly spiced foods and excessive smoking) he suffered from among other afflictions a plague of boils; and those coming near to him were soon aware of his lack of personal hygiene. He was usually at odds with his family, especially in religious disagreements; when he was only twenty his father died taking him to task for his extravagance; and his mother, worn down by repeated requests for money, told him bluntly that she wished he would start accumulating capital instead of writing about it. His wife, Jenny, of Scottish–Prussian origins (said to be descended from an Earl of Argyll) had a cheerless existence, weighed down by an unhappy family and ever prevalent shortage of money. She was faced with every humiliation – frequent visits to pawnbrokers and eviction into the street for non-payment of rent. She bore Marx seven children – four who died in childhood and three frustrated daughters, longing to escape into marriage or careers, but compelled to stay at home for household or clerical duties. Two of them were to commit suicide. Jenny was also to become aware of her husband's infidelity. Included in the household was an unpaid maid-of-all-work known as Lenchen who bore the brunt of domestic chores and who also bore Marx a son. Freddy, as he was called, was never acknowledged by Marx who was at pains to conceal him and he was boarded out into a working-class foster home, allowed to visit his mother occasionally, but always by the tradesmen's entrance and confined to servants' quarters. Subsequently he qualified as an engineer in King's Cross.

For as long as she could Jenny strove to 'keep the pot boiling' in a discordant home, but it became too much for her, especially after she became a victim of smallpox which ruined her good looks. 'Every day,' wrote Marx, 'my wife tells me she wishes she was lying in her grave.' And yet all was not bleak despair in the Marx household. As well as a political philosopher, writing long unreadable tracts on such subjects as the Theory of Value, Marx was a poet composing freely on romantic themes. He also had a sense of humour of a sort capable at times of jovial company which would raise morale. But joy did not come easily to him and he was not renowned for good cheer. He was to die in 1883 at the age of sixty-four. Jenny preceded him by two years.

Few writers have had such an impact on history. *Das Kapital* was to become a sacred text, the inspiration of revolution everywhere. After the Second World War with its victory of Communism over Fascism, Marxism was to spread like wildfire into Eastern Europe, China, Indo-China and Cuba among others. The world was to be saturated with Marxist doctrine and the name of Marx held in great reverence especially among the working class from whom he had so distanced himself.

Marx was not to survive to witness the fearsome crimes committed in his name – the reign of terror set up in Russia by Stalin, his massacre of peasants (Mujiks) and execution of rivals under the pretext of 'purifying' Communism; the mass murders of Mao Tse-Tung in China and the elimination of one third of the population of Cambodia by Pol Pot to bring about a society of submissive peasants. What would have been Marx's attitude to these atrocities?

Marxism was to fade away, replaced by an oligarchy of rampant capitalism. A new age had arrived. For how long would it last?

HENRIK IBSEN

(1828–1906)

'FRIENDSHIP AN EXPENSIVE LUXURY'

At the end of the 19th century the theatre in France was in need of change. For years it had been dominated by impassioned melodramas in declaratory semi-operatic style, rife with murder, rape and embattlement. At the peak of this drama was the great Sarah Bernhardt with magnificent presence and wondrous voice, capable of playing parts varying from Cleopatra at her most sensuous to Joan of Arc (when in her fifties and a great grandmother) and even Hamlet (when she was nearly sixty). To many she was incomparable. Lord Curzon, the most intellectual of British cabinet ministers, wrote of her: 'she was by far the most gifted actress I ever saw. She could range over the entire diapason of sound and feeling from savage fury to unutterable tenderness and despair.' To Max Beerbohm, wit and caricaturist, she was 'the epitome of majesty, awe and wonder.' And yet the feeling was growing that drama of that type – improbable plots and fantastic characters – had become dated. All was outward show with no attempt to analyse the characters portrayed and delve into their innermost thoughts.

Innovation was needed, and when this came it was from an unlikely source. Norway at that time was considered a backwater of Europe. For centuries it had been under the suzerainty of Denmark and had little cultural heritage of its own. The prevalent language was Danish; Norwegian was hardly more than a provincial dialect. Yet it was from this that a revolution in European theatre was to come, the most part from the talent, some would say genius, of one man.

Henrik Ibsen was born in 1828 in the remote Norwegian seaport of Skien. There conditions were rough, in some ways not far from primitive, abounding in eerie legends and weird superstitions. His father, Knud, descended from a long line of sea captains, was a merchant of varying fortunes (including bankruptcy), and at times his family was seriously impoverished. Ibsen, however, was able to stay at school until he was sixteen by which time he had acquired literary tastes; but then the only job he could find was as assistant to an apothecary, which he had to endure for six years; but he maintained his interest in literature and was to write a number of lightweight pieces – poems, sketches, reviews – none of which were to see the light of day. He persevered in spite of failure and disappointment; and when he was twenty-two he was taken into the first Norwegian language theatre in Bergen at a minimal salary, doing all kinds of jobs, many of the humblest sort, but gaining invaluable experience of the theatre and its ways. His first play *Catiline* was put on stage but soon taken off.

In 1858 when he was thirty he married Suzannah Thoreson, described by one observer as 'strong minded but entirely lacking in humility and womanly love.' In old age he wrote that 'marriage sets the mark of slavery on everyone.'

However, the marriage was to last to his death in spite of stormy passages. Some of these were severe. One witness wrote of 'Ibsen in the desperate situation of finding himself married to a woman he did not love and no reconciliation possible... and they waged war on each other ceaselessly.'

Gradually Ibsen gained a reputation. The plays he wrote, if not staged, were published and read by an increasing number of people. A critical break came in his thirties when he was awarded a grant for foreign travel as a result of which he was to spend twenty-nine years abroad, first in Italy and then in Germany.

During this time he wrote the greatest of his plays including *A Doll's House* (1879), *Wild Duck* (1884), *The Master Builder* (1892), *Hedda Gabler* (1890), and in a different vein the mock heroics of *Peer Gynt*. It was these which were to bring him worldwide fame and a dominating position in the theatre. Their aim was to make people think, to edify and awaken rather than just to entertain. In brief, they brought realism into the theatre. They were not of great heroes and full-blooded drama but of modern social problems such as the power of money and the oppression of women. They were intended to question and undermine entrenched beliefs and generally accepted moral principles and set people free from the prejudices and inhibitions of former times. The plays in which he was so successful were written in plain prosaic language with no polemics or high-flown histrionics. They showed that propaganda was most effective when it was not too obvious – insidious and oblique rather than ranting and raving.

When Ibsen returned to Norway in 1891 at the age of sixty-three he was welcomed as a national hero who had brought the country great renown, and there were celebrations of all sorts in his honour; but he was not cut out for such a role. To the contrary, he became increasingly graceless and misanthropic. For most of the time he kept himself to himself and attended public functions grudgingly and churlishly. He seemed to delight in giving offence – especially towards those to whom he was most indebted. He was especially mean and heartless towards his family. For forty years he had had no contact with his father who was financially stressed and he did little to help his legitimate son, Sigurd, on his way. His illegitimate son, Hans Jacob, whom he had fathered in his youth by a housemaid, he tried to ignore. He was of considerable wealth by then but showed few signs of being ready to share it.

Politically he was volatile and unconstructive, obsessed with the idea that minorities were always more liable to be in the right than majorities. He belonged to no political party. He was always ready to demolish and replace with something new; but was never clear as to exactly what. He was a strongly proclaimed egalitarian, but had little contact with the working classes.

Ibsen then did little to make himself popular, an ungenerous family man with few friends, (describing friendship as 'an expensive luxury') and a repellent public image; and conspicuous unattractive traits such as a passion for medals which he was at pains to be awarded and was to wear on every possible occasion. He was also possessed of irrational fears, being terrified by any sort of accident such as tiles falling off a roof onto him or a dog biting him or a boat sinking under him. He also had an obsession about his clothes, taking an hour each morning to dress and carrying in his top hat a mirror to check all was in place.

Yet in spite of his transgressions Ibsen was always to be highly respected. Honours continued to pour in and his plays were usually sell-outs second only to Shakespeare.

Enthusiasm, however, was not unanimous. There were those who found his works unintelligible and unappealing.

Were their long dialogues in commonplace language, devoid of wit or humour, to be thought on a par with the poetry and dramas of Shakespeare? *A Doll's House* and *A Wild Duck* with *Hamlet* and *Macbeth*? And were those brought up on the great deeds of gods and goddesses to be enthralled by the psychological hold-ups of middle-class Norwegians? But his influence was to be widespread and long lasting. In some circles he was always to be held as a monument of enlightenment.

In 1900 at the age of seventy-two he had the first of a series of strokes which made all work impossible. He was to live for a further six years in which he despaired and raged furiously at his helplessness, making life fraught and at times hazardous for those who came to minister to him. He died in 1906 and at his state funeral there were crowds of pilgrims who had come from far afield to pay homage to him as a saviour and fount of all wisdom.

LEO TOLSTOY

(1828—1910)

'UNIVERSAL SPIRITUAL RESURGENCE.'

Few writers have so enthralled their readers as Leo Tolstoy. To he himself, however, of more importance was an innate feeling of a universal spiritual resurgence which he would lead to a kingdom of heaven on earth. He was convinced that it was for this that his life was to be devoted. His writing was secondary.

As a prophet of God, Tolstoy's upbringing was far removed from that of Jesus Christ. The latter had allegedly been born in a manger and brought up in comparative poverty the son of a carpenter, whereas the former was a scion of a Russian aristocratic family who would in time become the owner of an estate of 4000 acres and over 300 serfs. His father had been a wastrel who had frittered away much of the estate, but his mother was made of sterner stuff, the daughter of Prince Volkonsky, one of the highest degree, and it was from her that he inherited the estate of Yasnaya Polyana in his early twenties in preference to his three elder brothers who, like their father, were considered inadequate. As a young man Tolstoy had no particular attributes: he was not notably good looking nor clever and as then of little driving force or ambition; but conspicuous was a consuming sexual appetite over which he exercised little restraint. He was also an inveterate gambler, unable to resist the lure of the gaming tables and losing large sums of money. He was not held in great repute and was often overcome with self-disgust, but this did not hold him back for long, and there was no question of him renouncing his title or withdrawing from high society.

At the age of twenty-three after considering various careers he drifted into the army. From the start he was an unconventional soldier, with little regard for regimental customs and disciplines. Although a loner he commanded respect and was always ready for the front line when there was a prospect of battle; although neglectful of routine military chores his courage was never doubted.

It was during Tolstoy's five-year army career (included a spell fighting British, French and Turkish forces in the Crimean War in the long drawn-out siege of Sevastopol) that he made the vital discovery of his unique gift for literature. In 1852 at the age of twenty-four his first book *Childhood* was published and was well received. In 1860 he set to work on his opus magnum *War and Peace*. The first part of this was finished in 1865 and the full work completed four years later.

By then he was seven years into his traumatic marriage to Sonya Behr. The wedding had occurred in 1862 when Tolstoy was thirty-four and Sonya, the daughter of a well-to-do doctor, sixteen years younger. At the time she could have had little idea of what she was letting herself in for. Tolstoy was not then rich nor recognised as a literary genius, but a ravenous sex maniac, addicted to gambling and with views on women similar to those of an oriental sultan.

Portrait of Leo Tolstoy, 1855 (photo) / Private Collection
Prismatic Pictures / Bridgeman Images

On becoming engaged, Tolstoy, feeling that all should be an open book between husband and wife, gave her a copy of his diaries for the last fifteen years containing details of his erotic affairs with all sorts of women and his numerous illegitimate children who had passed out of sight, left to their own resources. In return Sonya gave Tolstoy a copy of her greatly less explicit diaries. This was hardly a good start to a marriage which was to have many torments. Later Sonya was to say that he was incapable of person to person love, only of a loudly proclaimed one for all humanity. His demands on Sonya, however, were voracious and in twenty-two years she had twelve pregnancies. Finally, he publicly renounced sex and said that he and Sonya would live as brother and sister, which Sonya regarded as a personal insult and led to a bitter estrangement.

In the years that followed Sonya bore the brunt of Tolstoy's rages and obsessions. Always she was a soothing influence and attempted to maintain some kind of order in the household, which was to prove an impossible task. Increasingly Tolstoy came to look on marriage as a curse preventing him from achieving his main purpose in life – to discover its general meaning and bring about the moral transformation of society. And it was not only marriage but all women who stood in his way. He might not be able to resist them, but he declared that they 'were the cause of all sensuality, indulgences and frivolity', and that the company of women was an unavoidable social evil and men should keep away from them as much as possible, and that if this was not possible then prostitution ('an honourable calling') was preferable to marriage, which he strongly urged young women to avoid at all costs. In keeping the peace Sonya soon realised that Tolstoy had to be kept writing. When thus employed he was at his most reasonable; and to this end she would spend laborious hours making fair copies of his almost illegible manuscripts.

It was moreover not only women who stood in the way of Tolstoy's great moral purpose. The same applied to his writing. *War and Peace* was written between 1865 and 1869 and *Anna Karenina* between 1875 and 1877 and these had brought him fame and riches along with troubled souls, confused visionaries and cranks of all sorts crowding in on him seeking guidance and words of wisdom, which he was only sometimes ready to give. He was always to insist, however, that writing stories was stupid and shameful and could not bring him the moral leadership he sought.

In Politics Tolstoy's views were wild and deleterious. He had no time for gradual democratic development. What was needed was a convulsive upheaval brought about by himself. Parliaments he despised as doing more harm than good and an infringement on personal liberty. If his views had been more reasonable, such was his reputation, that he might have had a palliative effect on the Bolshevik Revolution when it came with such massive death and destruction, and more especially the elimination of the Mujiks, the peasants nearest to his heart – put to death, herded off to the salt mines of Siberia or left to die of starvation following the failure of the communist collectivisation of agriculture.

Tolstoy was no theologian, picking at random from the New Testament according to his personal choice and ready to override God. He cut out the mystic, and in 1901 was excommunicated from the Greek Orthodox Church for denying the divinity of Christ. He became strongly drawn towards the doctrines of Rousseau, saying that he and the Gospels had been the two great and healthy influences in his life.

In a turbulent life it is likely that his greatest torment was Yasnaya Polyana, his massive estate. With inherent egalitarian instincts this caused him strong offence and he longed to be rid of it. The serfs weighed heavily on him and he had in mind at times sweeping reforms, including emancipation, but these came to nothing, and when in 1861 serfs were set free by decree of Czar Alexander II, he was resentful that he had had no part in it.

At times he became deeply ashamed of living in luxury while others starved and he would turn himself into a peasant (in appropriate garb) performing menial tasks like sawing wood and pumping water and proclaiming the beauties of a healthy open-air life; but these obsessions did not last long.

At one time he became convinced that the solution to the problems of serfs lay in education and he devised a new system with himself doing some of the teaching (described later as the happiest days of his life); but like other bursts of enthusiasm they were not to survive, and he was to assert that 'children need no education whatsoever, and the more learned the man the stupider.' Way out as some of his opinions might have been, because of his novels they were always ensured widespread reverence.

Tolstoy's life ended in stark tragedy, steeped in ever increasing conflict, discord and deceit. None of his notions about saving humanity came to anything, his ideas ever more enmeshed and contradictory. His aversion to Sonya intensified and became, as he put it, 'a struggle to death.' This he recorded in secret diaries (hidden in a boot) venting his venom. These Sonya discovered and described them as 'untrue, distorted and fabricated', though she felt obliged to make a fair copy of them all the same.

Tolstoy's tragedy was largely self-inflicted. He grew ever more egotistical, treating women despotically and blaming them whenever anything went wrong. As well as the secret diaries there was the influence of Vladimir Chertkov, an ex-guards officer who had somehow insinuated himself into the family circle and established a hold over Tolstoy in bitter opposition to Sonya, stirring up trouble whenever he could. Tolstoy's last coup just before he died in 1910 was to make a new will leaving all his copyrights to his youngest daughter Alexandra with Sonya omitted – she who had struggled so desperately to keep the family together and the estate in some sort of order.

Tolstoy's life was a blend of triumph and tragedy. His name will live live on through his literature; but his life story was less marvellous – hardly a shining example of beneficence and high-mindedness; and his dream of founding a 'universal spiritual resurgence' came to nothing. With his prodigious gifts, he might have been expected to have achieved more.

BERTRAND RUSSELL

(1872—1970)

Bertrand Russell was a phenomenon – an academic of world renown, an active and controversial politician and a prolific writer and speaker on innumerable subjects (among others mathematics, logic, relativity, atheism and disarmament). Words, always fluent and articulate, poured from him in torrents; so too did ideas, some wise and well-reasoned, some erratic and extravagant. In the course of his life of ninety-seven years – from the Golden Jubilee of Queen Victoria to the explosion of the first hydrogen bomb – he wrote some seventy books and pamphlets, lectured at various universities, and founded several protest movements (the Campaign for Nuclear Disarmament and the International War Crimes Committee). He was, besides the grandson of a prime minister, a peer of the realm (3rd Earl Russell) although he did not use the title.

Russell was born in 1872 and at the age of four with the death of both parents became an orphan, and was then brought up in the home of his grandfather, the first Earl Russell, who as Lord John Russell had steered the Great

Reform Bill of 1832 through the House of Commons. In the eighteen seventies he was living in a grace-and-favour house in Richmond Park accorded him by Queen Victoria. Here the dominant influence was Russell's grandmother, a formidable lady of strong puritanical principles who saw to it that Russell had a strict religious upbringing, although this did not prevent him at the age of eighteen from declaring himself an unbeliever. For the rest of his life he had no faith in a supreme beneficent creator nor, indeed, in any external forces. He was convinced that humanity was the one and only guiding force and determining factor. In his childhood Russell was spared the rigours of a boarding school and had been educated at home by a succession of governesses and tutors which resulted in him getting a scholarship to Trinity College, Cambridge where in 1893 at the age of twenty-one he was listed as Seventh Wrangler[1] in the Mathematical Tripos, and this was followed by the grant of a fellowship. By then he had developed a love for mathematics: 'I like mathematics', he wrote, 'because it is not human – Mathematics possesses not only truth but supreme beauty – a beauty cold and austere, like that of sculpture without appeal to any part of our weaker nature, sublimely pure and capable of a stern perfection such as only the greatest art can show.'

It soon became clear that Russell had unconventional ideas about subjects other than mathematics. Throughout the First World War he was an outspoken pacifist propounding vociferously that Britain should never have been drawn into it; for the war would have been over much sooner and Europe would have been spared the immense loss of life which came from four years of slaughter with millions killed, wounded, gassed and demoralised; more than that there would have been no rise later of the communists in Russia

---

1 Candidate with highest marks.

nor the Nazis in Germany. This was a dangerous course of action in war time when the least deviation from the patriotic line could cause hysterical anger. Russell was to be violently abused, deprived of his Trinity fellowship and committed to prison. In 1916 he was put on trial for writing an article in defence of a conscientious objector and when found guilty was fined £100 which he refused to pay so that his furniture was distrained. Not discouraged he was in trouble again in 1918 when he wrote a convoluted and nonsensical article, the gist of which was that American troops would be ineffective against the Germans as their only experience of warfare was the intimidation of strikers in the United States. For this he was charged under the Defence of the Realm Act with 'having in a printed publication made certain statements likely to prejudice His Majesty's relations with the United States of America'. Found guilty, he was sentenced to six months in prison which proved to be not so gruesome as expected as he was placed in First Division (as opposed to hard labour in Second) where he was allowed privileges including as many books as he liked to read and write. Later he could say that he found prison 'in many ways quite agreeable.'

In the last years of the war and afterwards Russell confronted the communist revolution in Russia. It seemed probable that like most left-wing intellectuals he would rejoice in it, but he didn't. In 1920 on a visit to Russia he was accorded an hour-long interview with Lenin who did not impress him. He likened him to 'an embodied theory, an intellectual aristocrat who despised the populace'. For Stalin he had nothing but contempt — 'a monster out for world domination'. He was in no doubt that Communism with its collectivisation of farming and mass killing of the mujiks by starvation, the forced labour camps and the purge of political rivals, was a force for evil.

In the inter-war years Russell's books on mathematics and philosophy were well received, although in these he made no concessions to popular language. These subjects were for the chosen few to be treated in their own arcane idiom. They were not for the common throng. But among fellow philosophers he was not always appreciated. Ludwig Wittgenstein whom Russell described as 'the most perfect example I have ever known of genius as traditionally conceived; passionate, profound, intense and dominating', nevertheless said of his book, *Conquest of Happiness* that it was 'unbearable'; and another wrote off *Human Knowledge* as 'the patter of a conjuror.' However, his *History of Western Philosophy*, which came after the war, proved to be a universal bestseller. In his works arrogance was not avoided, and some of his opinions caused outrage as for example that American mothers were guilty of 'instinctive incompetence' and 'children should be sent to boarding schools to get them away from mother love.' There were those who could not take him seriously and looked on him not so much as a learned professor as 'a mischievous crank' who bore out the judgement of the Roman governor Festus about St Paul that 'much learning had made him mad.'[2]

In Russell's early life the most active and vehement of political movements was that of women's suffrage. Russell was a supporter of votes for women as he was for other women's rights in such as divorce and co-education. But he was not a wholehearted believer in the equality of men and women and his attitude to women tended to be condescending (though he married four of them). As he put it bluntly: 'scientific attitudes to life can scarcely be learned from women.'

In 1894 he married Alys Whitall of American birth and a member of the Society of Friends (Quakers). She was a gentle

---

2   *The Acts of the Apostles* chapter 6.

Bertrand Arthur William Russell

Bridgeman Images

and supportive wife,[3] and during most of their marriage of sixteen years he was a reasonably faithful husband but in 1911 when he was nearly forty, he fell in love with Lady Ottoline Morrell, a notorious London hostess, and sought a divorce. By then his views on the sanctity of marriage had changed. At first he had been on the whole straitlaced, maintaining that logic, reason and moderation could sort out emotional problems, but later, when put to the test, he was to find that they were helpless. He had spates of emotion he could not control and his conduct became increasingly unbridled. In 1914 he had a shameful affair with a Helen Dudley from Chicago whom he brought to London but had then deserted on the outbreak of the First World War, remarking callously that this had killed his passion for her. She subsequently became insane. By 1916 he had acquired as mistress another London socialite, Lady Constance Malleson. In 1920 after a divorce from Alys he married Dora Black, a strong feminist who basically disapproved of marriage but was to bear him two children, John and Kate. After marriage to Dora for fourteen years Russell fell for Patricia Spence (usually known as Peter), an undergraduate who had come to look after his children. After a disordered and acrimonious divorce from Dora in 1935 he married Peter. This marriage was to last for fifteen years and for most of this time they were happy and well disposed, but in old age Russell's sex life ran amok.

Dispassionate analysis and openness went by the board, replaced by furtiveness and duplicity. He slept around, often indiscriminately. Whenever his head and heart were in conflict it was the latter which predominated. In 1952, when he was eighty, he and Peter divorced, and Russell took as his fourth and final wife Edith Finch, an American teacher, sympathetic

---

[3] But not, as he later recalled, 'what his grandmother would call a lady.'

and down to earth who took care of him for the last eighteen years of his life.

The outbreak of the Second World War in 1939 found Russell in America where he had just been barred from a job because of a charge brought against him of being among other things 'lecherous, libidinous and bereft of moral fibre.' This was upheld by the Mayor of New York on the grounds that he was 'an alien atheist and exponent of free love.' He was to spend much of the Second World War in America, at times severely stretched financially. But he was to be no pacifist, as he had been during the First World War; he was fully committed to the destruction of Nazism.

At the end of the war, however, he was to speak out forcefully because of his dread of Soviet Communism and its expansion into eastern Europe. In doing so his pacifism became blended with belligerence, and he was driven into extremist views. He urged the use of force to coerce the Russians while the United States had superiority in nuclear weapons. 'Terrible as a new world war would be,' he declared, 'I still for my part would prefer it to a world Communist empire.'

He was to fluctuate from one extremist view to another – from 'better dead than red' to an abhorrence of all nuclear weapons and the need for their total destruction. In 1953 he was to declare brazenly that he had never supported a preventative war against Russia, and this was a communist 'invention'. When confronted with his earlier pronouncements he could bring himself to say: 'It is entirely consistent with what I think now ... I had in fact completely forgotten that I had ever thought a policy of threat involving possible war was desirable.' And later: 'At the time I gave this advice I gave it so casually without any real hope that it would be fulfilled, that I soon forgot I had given it.'

His dread of nuclear weapons was to intensify. In 1958 he

founded with Canon John Collins the Campaign for Nuclear Disarmament (CND) with demonstrations in Trafalgar Square and Easter marches to Aldermaston in Berkshire where atomic weapons were believed to be stored. In 1961 at the age of eighty-nine he was sent to prison for two months for 'inciting members of the public to commit a breach of the peace in protest movements against nuclear weapons.' At its height CND was to attract wide popular support. In 1981 both the Labour Party and the Trade Union Congress were to vote in favour of unilateral nuclear disarmament.

Ralph Schoenman, an American of some intellectual standing (philosophy graduate of Princeton and the London School of Economics) had been involved in Russell's civil disobedience campaigns and became a strong admirer which, to some extent, Russell reciprocated so that Schoenman became his amanuensis and often his mouthpiece, taking it on himself to announce to the world Russell's views on various subjects, writing letters in his name and organising his visitors. Schoenman was also adept in the matter of finance so that under his ægis Russell became a rich man. Russell was later to say that he had 'never taken Ralph as seriously as he liked to think I had. I was fond of him in the earlier years, but I never looked upon him as a man of parts and weight and much individual importance', discarding him after six years as he might have shed one of his wives.

Russell was to go from one extremist view to another, and by the end of the nineteen fifties he had become a passionate anti-American. He had taken a strong aversion to what he called the 'capitalist imperialism of America', and asserted that 'unless it could be shaken there would be a complete collapse of civilisation.' His hostility became more intense when America became involved in the war in Vietnam. This had been stepped up by President J.F. Kennedy in 1961 when support was given to South Vietnam to prevent the spread of Communism in South East Asia. This policy was carried further by President Johnson and American forces were poured into Vietnam, amounting by 1966 to as many as 400,000 personnel. At the time of the Cuban missile crisis[4] Russell declared that 'we would all be dead in a week to please American madmen.' Kennedy and the British premier Harold Macmillan were denounced as murderers and 'about fifty times as guilty as Hitler, who had wanted to exterminate only Jews whereas they sought the extinction of mankind. They are the wickedest people that ever lived.' American soldiers were worse than Nazis and were alleged to have committed all kinds of atrocities. In 1966 Russell was instrumental in setting up an International War Crimes Tribunal to sit in judgement on them. In time, the war in Vietnam provoked widespread opposition and had to be abandoned. A ceasefire was agreed in 1973 and in 1975 all American forces were withdrawn, leaving Vietnam to the communists.

Bertrand Russell died in 1970 at the age of ninety-seven. His legacy to posterity was considerable – some seventy books, innumerable newspaper and magazine articles and countless lectures, talks and interviews. Few Englishmen have been so extensively publicised. As a mathematician and philosopher he was at the top of the tree, regarded throughout the world with great veneration. His views on other subjects were less well received. On politics they were erratic and changeable. At one stage he detested Stalinist Communism to the extent of seeming to advocate its suppression by nuclear force (while this might have been possible), later attacking the United

---

[4] In October 1962 Nikita Khrushchev, Russian head of state since the death of Stalin in 1953 ordered the setting up of ballistic missiles in Cuba (communist since the successful rebellion of Fidel Castro in 1959). These would be capable of reaching most American cities, and President Kennedy took a firm line against them which resulted in them being dismantled, but a nuclear war had become more of a reality than at any other time.

States viciously when that country attempted to prevent the spread of Communism in Vietnam.

Like other philosophers (notably Marx and Rousseau), Russell's private life was not exemplary – four wives, three somewhat neglected children and widespread adultery. However, his courage in expressing unpopular views regardless of consequences including bitter abuse and imprisonment must not be forgotten, nor his bright and entertaining company and generosity to those in need.

In extreme old age, Russell retired to a home in North Wales (Plas Penrhyn on the Portmeirion Peninsula) where he led a quiescent life.

In spite of erratic views and behaviour he was to be revered and regarded by many as the fount of all wisdom. Until the day of his death pilgrims from afar would arrive at Plas Penrhyn in the hope of enlightenment.

GEORGE ORWELL

(1903–1950)

'THE REAL DIVISION IS NOT BETWEEN CONSERVATIVES AND REVOLUTIONARIES BUT BETWEEN AUTHORITARIANS AND LIBERTARIANS.'

George Orwell (Eric Blair as he was then) was born in India in 1903. He came from a well-to-do family, his father a respected member of the Indian Civil Service. After a brief unhappy spell at Wellington College, Orwell was accepted as a King's Scholar at Eton. He was not, however, able to go to a university as his father's finances could not run to that. Instead he took the exam for the Indian Imperial Police in which he was successful although with no great distinction and little enthusiasm. He was posted to Burma.

At that time the British Empire covered nearly a quarter of the earth's surface – though it was soon to be brought down not so much by force of arms as by an emaciated figure in a loincloth weaving textiles by hand and deriving salt from the ocean by the most primitive of methods; such was the source of the power of Mahatma Gandhi. Orwell was not cut out to be a 'pukka sahib.' He was shocked by the idea of a master race and disgusted by the treatment meted out to the natives. He resigned from IIP after four years. As a result of these early experiences he became a passionate believer in the equality of man, and not a theoretical one on the sidelines but one in the thick of life among the poorest of the poor.

After his resignation it became necessary for him to earn a living by other means and these were not easily to be found. He knew he wanted to become a writer but there were few financial opportunities for this, and it became necessary for him to fall back on his parents' retirement home in Southwold, a seaside town in Suffolk where he was not in his element. He was bored stiff by the elderly genteel inhabitants and looked for less reputable company wherever it was to be found even among tramps and vagabonds in Vagrant Casual Wards (known as spikes). He was to become fascinated by life among the poorest, and to find out more about them he would mingle among them in an attire described by his friend Malcolm Muggeridge as 'proletarian fancy dress' (leather jerkin, corduroy trousers tied up with string which had been rolled in dirt and boots that had been roughed up).

Muggeridge, journalist and broadcaster, could not altogether take Orwell seriously, saying that he was 'lean and egotistical, honest and foolish, and resembling Don Quixote, a veritable Knight of Woeful Countenance.' When he was not masquerading as a tramp Orwell scrounged a living as best he could, sometimes as tutor, sometimes helping out with domestic duties in boarding houses, but he did not lose sight of his ultimate ambition of becoming a writer, and he dashed off a number of miscellaneous pieces, some of which were published.

In 1928 Orwell decided to visit Paris to see how the underclass ('Paris underneath Paris' as it was known) 'lived, starved and died.' He was to stay for eighteen months, for most of the time on the brink of starvation after he had been robbed of the money he had brought with him. Later he was to describe this as an opportunity rather than a disaster as it ensured he had to live in direst poverty which he had come there to experience including a three-week spell in the grim and terrible Hôpital Cochin where the poor went to die.

He found himself some sort of lodging (dirty and bug ridden) in the cheapest of hotels, Le Coq d'Or in the Latin Quarter where the old Etonian had diverse company which included among others out-of-work kitchen porters, lavatory attendants and scrubbing women as well as ci-devant Russian aristocrats, once living in palaces, now after the communist revolution finding refuge in filthy hovels or sleeping under the bridges of the Seine. With one of these known as Boris, once an officer in the Czarist army, a raffish character boasting he had once had more than two hundred mistresses, he became particularly friendly as together they suffered privations and frustrations, subsisting on a few centimes and desperately seeking jobs which could hardly ever be found. To stay alive both of them were compelled to pawn most of their clothing but not all as it was necessary to keep up appearances if they were to have any chance of finding jobs. This Orwell did eventually find in a smart hotel as a dishwasher (plongeur) in which he had to work for up to seventeen hours a day in gruelling and fetid conditions. From this he was to move to a newly opened restaurant where conditions proved to be even worse – 'all muddle, petty spite and exasperation.' He remarked later how monstrous it was that there was only an insubstantial partition between on one side kitchen staff toiling in squalor and chaos and on the other rich overfed customers attended by smarmy servile waiters.

Orwell's description of life in the Paris underworld was certainly lurid and he was later to hint that there may have been 'literary embellishments'; but he could not afford to be pornographic. The English readers for whom he intended to write were not ready for this yet.

Orwell returned to England in the expectation of a job looking after a mentally disabled patient but this proved illusory and it was necessary for him to exist in what he called some hole-in-corner way. The next five years were to be for him time in abeyance – keeping going but with no significant breakthrough. He continued to keep in contact with the poorest, with tramps in spikes and in London with such low life as pavement artists, organ grinders and sandwich men (those in between advertising posters). In 1932 he went hop picking in Kent with crowds of cockneys from London's East End and enjoyed their ribald humour. From his association with the poor he could not but admire the simple philosophy of some of them – feeling no self-pity, unashamed of their poverty and 'having the decency to be ungrateful' for any offering that might come their way.

During these years he did not give up on his ambition of becoming a writer, ready to put his hand to opportunities that might arise perhaps in the way of reviews or small news items. He also wrote two novels (*A Clergyman's Daughter* and *Keep the Aspidistra Flying*) which had some success but did not bring in enough finance to live on, and it was necessary for him to take on extraneous jobs so that at times he was to be found teaching in dim day schools (Hawthorn High School with fourteen pupils of which he was nominally headmaster), and at others as an assistant in a second-hand bookshop (Booklovers' Corner). But for none of these had he any enthusiasm; these were mere stopgaps on his way to literary distinction.

Orwell's fortunes were to change when he was brought

into contact with a new force in publishing, Victor Gollancz, Jewish, highly intelligent, forceful and with a genius for publicity, but also unscrupulous and a stranger to truth. Though both he and Orwell held left-wing views they differed in almost every other respect. Gollancz enjoyed great wealth and a high standard of living, waited on by an array of servants and lunching every day at the Savoy Grill; while Orwell lodged in doss-houses and stood in line for a slice of bread and margarine.

In all but name Gollancz was a communist, supporting Stalin in nearly everything he did including the show trials of innocent victims, maintaining that these were to purify rather than to purge. Like most left-wing intellectuals he was ready to put ideas before people. Orwell on the other hand was not prepared to believe communist propaganda at sight, only what he himself had witnessed personally. In spite of their differences Gollancz recognised Orwell's literary abilities. In 1933, although not liking some of its tone, he had allowed the publication of *Down and Out in Paris and London*, and he had further uses for him. He was in the process of forming the Left Book Club with the object of spreading left-wing literature, and Orwell could be useful for that.

1936 was to be an eventful year for Orwell. In the early winter months Gollancz commissioned him for a hefty fee to make a tour of the north of England, visiting industrial centres, coalmines and docklands and reporting on working conditions in them. To this Orwell agreed, insisting as usual on seeing things at their worst, which led him for a time to lodging in a tripe shop in Wigan, one of the most depressed areas, but this he could not take; the squalor, decay and especially the smell were too much for him and he had to move out. He had become perhaps unduly obsessed by smell, attaching significance to it wherever he went.

In an extensive tour his worst experience was descending a

coalmine and having to walk miles underground in a narrow passage only occasionally standing upright.[1] He was deeply shocked by casualty rates in coalmines, many being killed or seriously crippled each year as a result of accidents, explosions and flooding, and many more being blinded by coal dust. And these were the men who were the backbone of Great Britain's wealth and world power.

On his return south Orwell settled not in London but in a small farm-cum-shop-cum post office in a remote village in Hertfordshire. Wallington had thirty-five cottages, two pubs and a church. The farmhouse in which Orwell lived was semi-derelict – corrugated iron roof, defective drainage causing flooding, an outside lavatory which tended to get blocked and a minimum of modern conveniences (no electricity, running hot water nor telephone). But the rent was minuscule, barely 30/- a week, and Orwell was confident he could make a small profit on which he could live and get on with his writing; but this proved impractical. He had to have a wife and fortunately one was in the offing. He had known Eileen O'Shaughnessy for some time and they had become semi-engaged. Now he proposed to her formally and she accepted him. In June 1936 they were married in Wallington village church according to the rites of the Church of England in whose doctrines Orwell as a stalwart atheist had no beliefs but which he felt to be redolent of the English way of life.

Eileen was an intellectual lady, well connected and engaged in reading for a degree in educational psychology which she forsook in order to live with Orwell in Wallington. There she was to be the mainstay not only of all domestic matters but also of the shop and the farm (no more than vegetable patches, a few chickens and a couple of goats). This enabled Orwell to get on with his writing of *The Road to Wigan Pier*. The

---

[1] Especially difficult for one 6'3" tall.

marriage was to prove on the whole a happy one, although no children were to come from it; both parties were fond of each other and respected each other, although they seem to have agreed that neither was to be bound by marital fidelity. On this basis life proceeded reasonably smoothly – until July of 1936 when civil war broke out in Spain.

At the beginning of the 20th century Spain was lagging behind other European countries in political constitution, and was still an old fashioned semi-feudal aristocracy with power and wealth in the hands of the few. However, the winds of change were blowing. Movements for reform and a new order were becoming stronger, and in 1931 the Spanish king was forced to abdicate and Spain became a republic. Since then the clamour for change had grown louder and in 1936 a general election was held in which power was gained by an alliance of left-wing parties (Liberal, Socialist and Communist) which became known as the Popular Front. At this the forces of conservatism became alarmed and there was a revolt, mainly of Fascists and Monarchists, headed by the leaders of the army. At first the attitude of the government was weak and hesitant and the matter was taken lightly, but to the workers it was a signal for a general uprising. Trade Unionists and peasants formed themselves into workers' militias and demanded that the government should give them arms. At first the government held back from this but when the size of the movement became evident it complied. Spain was then in turmoil. Many of the militias were dominated by revolutionary parties and many atrocities occurred: factories were taken over by their workers, and agricultural land was nationalised and distributed to the peasants. Particular fury was vented on the Roman Catholic church as it was believed that it was essentially on the side of the old order and strongly opposed to change, and there were incidents of priests being murdered and churches desecrated and destroyed. For a time, the country was in chaos as in every city and province it was uncertain who was on the side of the elected government (Republicans) and who supported the rebels (so-called Nationalists). At first it seemed likely that the Nationalists might gain a quick victory. Their commander-in-chief, General Francisco Franco had come from North Africa with the Spanish Foreign Legion, crack troops of the Spanish army, and was being given support, particularly in air forces, by the Fascist dictators Hitler and Mussolini. However, the Republicans, although ill-armed and disorganised, were larger in number and fired with enthusiasm. Also they too were receiving help from abroad, from France and Russia (although this was to prove a mixed blessing). The British government was ambivalent, adopting a policy of non-intervention. It had no wish to see a Fascist dictatorship set up in Spain but was also anxious that the civil war should not escalate into a full-scale European war.

Although European leaders were to gain little credit for their actions and attitudes to the Spanish civil war, there were thousands of individuals who showed great heroism by going to Spain as volunteers to join in the fight against Fascism, and one of these was to be George Orwell.

In early life Orwell had shown no great interest in politics, but he became increasingly disturbed by the growth of Fascism in Italy and Germany, and when it threatened to spread into Spain, he felt action had to be taken. To him as to many others this was a moment of truth; the struggle of the Spanish workers was the struggle of all workers everywhere fighting for what they held dear – liberty, democracy and the right of ordinary people to a decent standard of living. He was determined to enter Spain to join in the fight, but this was to prove difficult.

The Spanish authorities kept a watchful eye on all those entering the country and were suspicious of Orwell.

He was not an orthodox communist. He was too much of a freewheeler. There would have been no objections if he could have produced a letter of recommendation from Harry Pollitt, General Secretary of the British Communist party; but this was not forthcoming. Pollitt was the most rigid of Stalinist communists. Of Stalin's recent show trials (judicial murders) he had written that they were 'a new triumph in the history of progress'; and of Orwell, middle class, and ex-Etonian, he was deeply distrustful. He was not a reliable supporter of the official party line, too inclined to go his own way. Pollitt's opposition meant that for the time being Orwell could not go to Madrid where an International Brigade was being formed. However, with help from the Independent Labour Party (ILP) he was able to cross the border and journey on to Barcelona.

Barcelona at that time had been taken over by workers and their unions. Strict equality and plain living were the order of the day: no smart clothes, shabby and half empty shops and the 'collectivisation' of small businesses.[2] The bourgeoisie were lying low or disguising themselves as proletarians; no titles, everyone addressing everyone else as 'comrade.' For a brief time, a genuine socialist society ensued.

But this situation was not replicated throughout Spain. The war might have ended sooner if there had not been bitter divisions among the Republican forces. There was hostility and distrust between Spaniards in Madrid (known as Castilians) and Catalans in Barcelona with separate language and culture, many of whom were bent on independence. The attitude of Stalin was, as might be expected, devious and treacherous. He might be opposed to Fascism, but he was even more opposed to another type of Communism known as

---

[2] Including prostitution, a notice being posted on the door urging men to 'treat women as comrades.'

anarchism,[3] which was closely associated with his arch-enemy Leon Trotsky, and he was anxious to see these obliterated (which in time he was able to achieve). The result of this was that he did not want to see the establishment in Spain of a communist government which might include Anarchists, and so his aim was to prop up the moderate Popular Front which he could keep under his thumb, and this meant him becoming a conservative influence in the civil war.

On arrival in Barcelona Orwell at first thought he could best serve anti-Fascism as a journalist writing vivid reports stirring up widespread support. He wanted to get to the front line as soon as possible and he found that the only way to do this was by joining a workers' militia known as POUM (Workers' Party of Marxist Unification) which was pre-eminently Anarchist. Here there was strict equality: no saluting, equal pay for all ranks and requests rather than orders which might be questioned. This was all very well, but it was no way to fight a war. Individual liberty was found to be incompatible with military discipline. There was a delay until enough recruits arrived to form a Centurion, as it was called, and these recruits were, to say the least, raw and unkempt – callow youths from the Andalusian countryside, full of enthusiasm and *esprit de corps*, but ignorant of military skills; little idea of how to use a rifle let alone a machine gun or hand grenade; and because of Castilian distrust of Catalans, armaments were in short supply. Orwell had to make do with an obsolete rifle and cartridges liable to be duds. Nevertheless, after a few weeks of basic training the Centurion marched off to the front in the Aragonese mountains to confront better trained Fascist forces only a few hundred yards away.

---

3   The essential belief of Anarchists was in a stateless society. A state was undesirable and harmful and laws unnecessary.

Conditions in the front were chaotic – dirt and disorder everywhere, infested by rats and lice, and bitter cold not to be withstood as the soldiery crouched round pathetic little camp fires, piled with as many clothes as they could put on. Action with the enemy was intermittent. Occasionally the opposing forces took pot shots at each other but they seldom reached their targets. The obsolete rifles were a menace, of more danger to those firing them than those being fired at; so too were the hand grenades, liable to explode unpredictably. Orwell was to reckon that more casualties were caused by faulty weapons than by fire from the enemy. He was to describe it as no more than pretence of a war. He endured this existence for three and a half months which he was to describe as the most futile of his life.

On leave in Barcelona, Orwell was to find a different city: gone was the classless society; money and privilege had re-established themselves. Shops, restaurants and brothels had been smartened up and were once again the haunt of the wealthy. He was reunited there again with Eileen who had managed to find a job with ILP, and he had hoped for some restful and peaceable days; but these were to be denied him when he became involved in street fighting between government forces and Anarchists which he found 'sickening and nerve racking.'

Back at the front he was not to be fortunate: within ten days he was shot through the throat by a sniper's bullet and only survived by millimetres.

In a military hospital he made a remarkable recovery. He had lost his voice but after four weeks this was restored, and he was back in Barcelona where he was out of danger from the Fascists but faced a more vicious enemy. Stalin had given orders that Anarchists were to be exterminated and this was being carried out ruthlessly by the Spanish government. Anarchists were accused of being secret agents of the Fascists (Franco's Fifth Column as they were dubbed) and its leaders were imprisoned, tortured and put to death. Included in this persecution was POUM, and its leaders were being rounded up, including foreigners who had enlisted in their ranks. A particularly monstrous case was that of a young Yorkshireman, Bob Smillie, son of a trade union leader who had given up a university career to fight Fascism. He was tortured to extract a confession and then horribly murdered.

At the realisation that extremists of the Left could be just as brutal and tyrannical as extremists of the Right, the Orwells fled Spain.

Once in safety Orwell looked back on his time in Spain without bitterness. He was aware that he and his rusty rifle had made no significant contribution to the defeat of Fascism and he had witnessed many atrocities – men being beaten up, falsely accused and imprisoned unjustly, but he still believed in the inherent goodness of the Spanish people, and he still believed in socialism – of a sort.

On his return to England he announced the book he was intending to write about his experiences in Spain, not omitting the brutality and duplicity of the communist dominated Spanish government, and how it was responsible for the slaughter of the Anarchists. This profoundly shocked orthodox communists and the great luminaries of the party, and left-wing publications would have nothing to do with it. Kingsley Martin, editor of the *New Statesman*, turned it down as being 'contrary to editorial policy'; Harold Laski, Labour heavyweight and professor in the London School of Economics, was cold and patronising, saying that Orwell was naïve and not prepared to pay the price of socialism; while Victor Gollancz, also condescending, said Orwell was too essentially middle class and could not be expected to have a deep-rooted understanding of socialism, and his book would do great harm to the fight against Fascism. Inevitably Harry

Pollitt joined in the onslaught in the columns of *The Daily Worker*, describing Orwell as a 'disillusioned little middle-class boy who, seeing through imperialism, decided to discover what socialism had to offer.'

But Orwell was not to be put off. He was able to find a small publisher (Secker & Warburg) who was prepared to publish *Homage to Catalonia* which came out in April 1938, laying bare fully and frankly the crimes of the communists, in imprisoning and killing the innocent and using Fascist methods for socialist ends. This caused further rage among orthodox communists. There were also ponderous articles from what Orwell called 'Bolshy professors', infinitely erudite but convoluted and unintelligible such as typically:

> *His innocence of Marxism–Leninism affected his judgement of all parties of the Spanish War, and since he was unaware of modern socialist dialectic and its tropes he was unable to examine them via a critical comparison with empirical reality.*[4]

By mid-July Orwell and Eileen had settled back in Wallington Farm, feeding ducks and chickens and milking nanny goats. While they were away the farm had been left in the care of Orwell's aunt Nellie, a lady of no great competence, mainly interested in Esperanto,[5] who had let things go so that conditions had become chaotic and needed special efforts to restore some sort of order. The burden of this fell, as usual, on Eileen while Orwell devoted himself to his writing in which he had become obsessed, determined as he put it, to 'spill the Spanish beans.' But this had to be abandoned when his health broke down, which was not surprising. He had become

---

4   Quoted from *Orwell's Nose* by J. Sutherland, Reaktion Books 2016.

5   Artificial international language.

overstrained. He had nearly died from pneumonia in 1933, suffered from great privation and a serious wound in Spain in 1937, had written six books in six years, and was suspected of tubercular infection. His brother-in-law and a distinguished surgeon, Laurence O'Shaughnessy, found for him a high-class sanatorium, Preston Hall in Kent, where he was to spend five and a half months followed by a winter in the warm climate of Marrakesh.

By then the prospect of a European war had become more imminent. After leaving Spain and seeing what a disastrous civil war there had been, Orwell was inclining towards pacifism. The pressures for war, it seemed to him were great – big business looking for big profits, Jews seeking suppression of anti-Semitism, communists out to spread their doctrines and Fascists to expand their frontiers. However, by 1939 he had no doubts that Nazidom had to be crushed, and he would have liked to enlist for military service, but his physical condition prevented this. He had to be content with the Home Guard.

During the war he was to have several jobs. At first he was taken on by the BBC as a talks assistant in the Indian Section of the Empire Service, steady and well paid but it did not suit him; he was subject to too many rules and regulations and interference from censors. There was also evidence that listeners in India were few in number. He was glad to become literary editor of *Tribune*, a left-wing magazine at the head of whose board was the turbulent Labour member of Parliament Aneurin Bevan, with whom he struck up a friendship. The scene changed again when he met the wealthy and highly successful newspaper proprietor David Astor who employed him as a war correspondent in *The Observer* which saw him in the final stages of the fighting in Europe. Eileen also found war work in the Ministry of Food, broadcasting to housewives in *The Kitchen Front*, telling them how to make the most of meagre wartime rations. Their relationship remained loving in its way and they were drawn together closer when they adopted an illegitimate wartime orphan whom they named Richard Horatio Blair and to whom both became devoted. But in 1945 came tragedy when Eileen in the course of an operation for hysterectomy died while under an anaesthetic. A devastated Orwell could not see how he could possibly manage without her – especially with a baby boy to look after. As it happened rescue came, as it had often done before, from his sister Avril who became a stand-in mother and housewife.

In 1943 Orwell wrote the book which was to make him world famous. From what he had witnessed in Spain he was convinced that Stalinist Communism was undistinguishable from Fascism, and he was determined to expose it. It could not be described as socialist and was debasing true socialism as practised in England. He had the idea of an animal fantasy when he saw a small boy whipping a large carthorse when it proved recalcitrant, and it occurred to him that the relationship of humankind to animals was similar to that of the mighty towards the downtrodden, and from this he was to create an extraordinary work of imagination in matchless English prose.

The revolution in Manor Farm, as it was originally called, began when an elderly prize boar, known as Old Major, had a vivid dream about mankind and animals. At present the lives of animals were miserable, laborious, short and geared entirely to the needs of Man; but if Man was to be overthrown there would come for animals an age of bliss, dignity and plenty. He could not tell when this would happen. It might be in the distant future, but in the event it was to come all too soon. Farmer Jones, who owned Manor Farm, was in trouble. He had had financial misfortunes and taken to drink. In consequence the farm had become run down and disorganised: routine tasks were neglected, and animals went unfed.

One Midsummer's Eve Mr Jones came home roaring drunk and went to sleep leaving the farm in chaos. This was too much for the hungry animals and they rose in rebellion. To their surprise they carried all before them: Mr and Mrs Jones and the farm staff were expelled, and the animals found themselves in possession of the farm. Leadership was then needed to take charge of a new regime and this fell to two formidable and dominating pigs, Napoleon and Snowball who proceeded to give orders and allot duties. At first all went swimmingly; everyone was filled with revolutionary fervour, revolutionary songs were bawled out with gusto, all old quarrels were forgotten, and it was generally accepted that unity was strength. Life in Animal Farm, as it was to be renamed, would be simple, plain and rigorous, and there would be strict equality in all matters, all working to the limits of their ability in the hopes of a new and glorious world.

But difficulties were soon to arise. Food ran short, and workers went hungry. There was also a bitter quarrel between Snowball and Napoleon, resulting in the former being driven into exile and the latter becoming a harsh and ruthless dictator. His word was law and the slightest sign of revolt was stamped out while he assumed ever greater powers and became ever more removed from the rank and file. He and his gang were to hold on to power by a barrage of lies, forced confessions and summary executions. Faithful old retainers of lesser intelligence and willpower were bamboozled into submission. Old ideals like never to make use of money, have no dealings with human beings and the banning of alcohol were put aside or revised for the benefit of the ruling clique. All animals were still proclaimed equal but some were 'more equal than others.' Conditions were worse than they had ever been under Farmer Jones.

Animal Farm was not an exact representation of the Russian revolution, but it was easily recognisable as such, and for that reason it was not possible for the book to be published in 1943 in the middle of the war with Germany when Russia was bearing the brunt of the fighting and had just won a decisive victory at Stalingrad. Criticism of Russia in general and Stalin in particular was virtually banned, especially by what Orwell scornfully called the 'literary intelligentsia.' Orwell was to relate that it was then easier to criticise Churchill than Stalin. And so the book had to go into cold storage until the end of the war when it was greeted with great acclaim. 'Matchlessly sharp and fresh...The clearest and most compelling English prose style this century,' wrote John Carey in the *Sunday Times*. 'Orwell's courage and Integrity shine from every page,' was written in the *Daily Telegraph*. By then the scales were beginning to fall from the eyes of the hide-bound socialist elite.[6] The Nazi–Russo treaty of alliance in 1939 had shaken them profoundly as would the invasion of Hungary in 1956.

In 1946 Orwell made a start on the second of his great masterpieces. *Nineteen Eighty-Four* was to be a grim and terrifying book. In Airstrip One, a province of Oceania, life was totally dominated by a brooding underworld power known as Big Brother. There, old values of loyalty, honesty and truth had been abandoned to be replaced by fear, hatred and suspicion. Essential beliefs were overturned: love became hate, war became peace, the price of freedom betrayal. Life for the ordinary citizen was indeed horrific: gone were the usual pleasures; the main ones in this fictional world spying on and denouncing one's neighbour. Ever present were Newspeak, doublethink, and Thought Police, lurking everywhere in every nook and cranny, even from the air in helicopters, ready to pounce on any sign of disloyalty which might result

---

[6] Both Victor Gollancz and Harold Laski came near to nervous collapses when they realised the extent of their error.

in death or disappearance (vapourisation as it was known). Individuals were reduced to subservient dummies incapable of independent thought.

In the midst of this barren existence came Winston Smith, an employee of the Ministry of Truth, engaged in rewriting the past to the glorifying of Big Brother. For rebellious thoughts and a secret love affair with a fellow worker, Winston paid a fearsome price. Brutally arrested and taken off to the dreaded Room 101, the torture chamber of the Thought Police, the tortures inflicted on Winston were spelled out remorselessly. Orwell recounted them in full, and it seemed at times to savour them.

Winston's tormentor set out to convince him that he was not being punished but rather cured, made ready for life under Big Brother. For this he had to be thoroughly purged of all his old ideas and filled with new ones, and these had to be genuine. Confession alone was not enough. There had to be nothing of the martyr for later generations to idolise. It was a pressure Winston found impossible to resist.

Written when Orwell was in his death throes, *Nineteen Eight-Four* required a tremendous effort. His health was deteriorating steadily, and on the Hebridean Island of Jura where he was living at the time, no typist was available to make a fair copy of his manuscript, a job previously undertaken by Eileen, so he had to undertake this task himself which he found a prodigious effort and one which must have shortened his life.

Orwell lived just long enough to see *Nineteen Eighty-Four* published and highly praised. His last years had been a losing battle with tuberculosis. He longed to go on living as he still had books he wanted to write. A few months before his death he had married Sonia Brownell, a loveless match more in the nature of a business agreement. It gave Sonia access to wealth, and it gave Orwell a competent manager to oversee his affairs, in particular to provide for his son Richard Horatio who was to be adopted by his sister Avril.

He died in January 1950 at the age of forty-six. Young as that was he had certainly made his mark. He was not a great novelist nor biographer, but as a literary stylist of the highest order; his political message was of vital importance and none could have made it more succinctly. In earlier life he had been denigrated by the intelligentsia as being naïve and unprincipled. For a time arid intellectuals like Karl Marx held sway, their convoluted doctrines treated like holy writ, but in the long run it was the straightforward narratives of the old Etonian which spread further and wider.

JEAN-PAUL SARTRE

(1905—1980)

EXISTENTIALISM

Few Frenchmen have had such a widespread influence on his fellow countrymen as Jean-Paul Sartre. Born into a well-to-do, middle-class family (his father a naval officer), he had a conventional upbringing, educated in the best lycées and then at the prestigious Ecole Normale Superieur from which he graduated with no great honours to become a schoolmaster in Le Havre, a somewhat low-key life which at that time (the 1920s) did not involve him in politics. He seemed unconcerned by the rise of Fascism in Germany, Italy and Spain nor in the persecution of the Jews, and took no part in France's Popular Front led by Leon Blum. For the time being he was immersed in philosophical studies which included logic, ethics and sociology.

One important friendship he formed at that time was with Simone de Beauvoir, an eminent scholar and philosopher (possibly superior to Jean-Paul) and strong feminist.

Throughout their lives they were to be close but did not marry. They went their own ways, meeting up occasionally and having great influence on each other. For a woman of her intellectual status it seemed strange she would be enslaved by Jean-Paul, acting at times as manager, nurse, mother and cook.

In spite of eyesight deficiency Jean-Paul was enrolled into the French army where he served in the meteorological section. When France was overrun by German armies in the spring of 1940 he became a prisoner of war for nearly a year, then released on the grounds that he was 'partially blind.' He made his way to Paris where he embarked seriously on a literary career, writing numerous novels, plays and various tracts. He also read voraciously, perhaps as many as three hundred books a year. It seems he was uninterrupted by the German authorities in Paris. He was non-political and as a philosopher regarded as harmless, even treated favourably. He was not a collaborator, but was not hostile to the Germans and did not join the Resistance. Later he was to declare: 'We have never been so free as we were under German occupation.'

From his literary activities, which he regarded as a substitute for religion, there was to emerge a philosophy which came to be known as Existentialism. Unlike some philosophers, Sartre did not consider philosophy to be beyond the reach of the general public; it could be made palatable if it was mixed with an element of fiction and some humour. It has always been difficult to define Existentialism exactly. Sartre himself once said that like Faith it cannot be explained, only lived. Essentially it was based on individualism in which men and women were entirely self-responsible and masters of their own souls, in contrast to the uniformity and regimentation of Fascism and Communism. People are free agents to be judged not by the views they hold but their actions – deeds not words. In post-war France this philosophy caught the mood of the moment which was ready for new and recondite ideas, partly perhaps as a reaction to the bleak and humiliating war years. Existentialism was to spread like wildfire and not only in France but in Europe too.

Although he did not marry, Sartre was certainly a womaniser, though he was hardly a romantic figure – undersized (5'6" tall), protuberant, nearly blind in one eye and usually unwashed and odoriferous. But there were those who were fascinated by him, by his flow of erudite talk, much of it incomprehensible but always fluent and spoken with conviction. He loved to flirt with young women (peripherals as he called them), and to conquer them and tame them like wild animals.[1]

It was not until 1948, when he was forty-three, that Sartre became involved in the political fray, drawn by left-wing revolutionary movements especially those of discontented youth. These he backed indiscriminately, regardless of their flagrant crimes. And so he strongly favoured Mao Tse Tung who murdered millions in his Cultural Revolution in China, as he did later the Khmer Rouge who exterminated perhaps as many as one third of the population in Cambodia in setting up a communist regime. He also backed the rebels in the French colony of Algeria, stating that 'each French person was responsible for collective crimes against the rebels,' and he might have been imprisoned for advocating civil disobedience, but General de Gaulle saw the danger of persecuting someone with his charisma. He loudly decried American 'crimes' in Vietnam and was an early visitor to Fidel Castro in Cuba where he fell under the spell of the adventurer Che Guevara whom he described as 'the most complete human being of all time.'

---

1   One of these, Arlette Elkaïm, he was to adopt as an unofficial daughter.

He had an uneasy relationship with Soviet Russia, as Marxism was in many ways the opposite of Existentialism, but he was a member of the Communist Party for four years during which time he turned a blind eye to the horrors of Stalinism and was even a vocal apologist. However, the Russian invasion of Hungary in 1956 to suppress a freedom movement was reason enough for him to quit the party. At home in France, Sartre – like Rousseau and Marx – was handicapped by his inability to establish rapport with the working class. He had little in common with factory workers and when the Renault car workforce went on strike he was rebuffed. He was only ever at ease with middle-class intellectuals.

When angry Parisian students took to the streets in 1968 he felt bound to put himself in their forefront even though he had renounced violence. Unconvincingly he recanted and let it be known that violence was at times unavoidable and the students were one hundred percent in the right. In these, as in other cases, Sartre showed himself to be no man of action, and he has been described, perhaps not altogether unjustly, as an armchair warrior, stirring up trouble and discontent but taking no part in it himself. And his interference often did more harm than good to those whose causes he espoused. His aim was always to support the oppressed against the oppressor, but this was not always clear cut; in Africa it often resulted in the oppressed fighting other oppressed with tin pot dictators at each other's throats in civil wars and massive slaughters.

In old age Sartre became an increasingly pathetic figure – nearly blind, often drunk and incomprehensible. He also found himself in financial straits. He had always been careless about money and was known for his generosity in disbursing financial aid to those in need; and he had never bothered about paying taxes, leaving this to his mother. The consequence was that enormous debts had accumulated so that at one stage he had not enough money to buy a pair of shoes. Although words still poured from him and there were still devotees ready to come to listen to him, he no longer held sway as the spiritual leader of thousands of young people and opposition mounted. There were those who regarded him as an enemy of society. His works were placed on the Vatican Index of Prohibited Books, and in the Kremlin he was known as 'a jackal with a typewriter' and 'a hyena with a fountain pen.'

When he died in 1980 at the age of seventy-five, disciples came from all over the world to witness his funeral in the Montparnasse Cemetery in Paris. But he was to pass from the scene, becoming known as 'a rebel without a cause.'

ALEXANDER SOLZHENITSYN

(1918—2008)

The life of Alexander Solzhenitsyn was a miracle. In spite of intense suffering and danger he survived to have a vital role in the demise of Communism and to become one of the most influential men in the world.

He was born in 1918 when the Russian Revolution was at its bloodiest and the civil war was being fought to the bitter end. His father had been an officer in the Czarist army and had fought gallantly against the Germans in the First World War, but had been killed in a hunting accident before Alexander was born, leaving his mother, Taissia, in penury and some danger from revolutionaries because of royalist connections. In the southern port of Rostov, where Alexander was brought up, he must have witnessed gruesome scenes – street battles, summary executions, bands of skeletal ravenous children roaming the streets and Ukrainian peasants evicted from their farms and loaded into cattle trucks about to be transported to Siberia.

At school Alexander was a top scholar and passed easily into university where, surprisingly, he read maths and physics, literature then being a sideline. At the time he became keenly interested in Marxism and was carried away by the theses propounded in *Das Kapital*, a copy of which he always had by him, even on his honeymoon. As becoming a staunch atheist, his marriage to Natalya Reshetovskaya had been plain and unromantic in a registry office with no one else present. Natalya, a chemistry student as well as a gifted pianist, shared his beliefs and for a brief time they were happy together.

With the German invasion of Russia in 1941, Alexander became strongly patriotic and was eager to join the army but from this he was prevented for a time because of a minor physical defect. He had to take a job as a schoolteacher, but after the initial heavy Russian defeats in 1941 shortage of manpower became acute. He was enrolled in the army and had a distinguished war record, rising to the rank of captain with two citations for bravery and competence.

Disaster was to come suddenly in 1945. By then German forces had been driven out of Russia into Poland and on into Germany, and urged on by Stalin, Russians were wreaking vengeance on German men, women and children – murder, massive rape, wanton destruction. Solzhenitsyn was shocked by this, and in a letter to a school friend criticised Stalin not only because of his encouragement of atrocities but also because of his practice of Communism which he thought untrue to Karl Marx. This was rash as it was picked up by the censors and he was arrested and falsely accused of plotting to overthrow the Soviet regime. On 9 February he was stripped of his commission, degraded, and dispatched to Lubyanka, the dreaded headquarters of NKVD, the secret police. There he was 'processed' – subjected to every kind of humiliation and crammed into a tiny windowless cell in which he couldn't lie down. With the coming of Victory in Europe Day in June 1945, he had hopes of amnesty and release. Instead, he who had been in the forefront of the battle had to watch the wild street rejoicings from a prison cell. In July, after a mockery of a trial he was sentenced to eight years of imprisonment, which he was to serve in full, for a few indiscreet words. For the duration of his sentence he was to be incarcerated in various 'correction camps'. In one of these, Marfino, thanks to his scientific knowledge he was for a time in comparative comfort, but in others conditions were grisly – hard manual work in sub-zero temperatures, bullied by guards and in close quarters with hardened criminals.

In 1952 he came close to death when a large swelling on his thigh was diagnosed as cancerous and required a major operation from which he was not expected to survive. But survive he did, and as a different man. He had had a spiritual awakening, leading to Communism giving way to Christianity.[1] He wrote later: 'First comes fight for survival, then discovery of life, then God.' His life then was set on a new course: gone was dialectical materialism, in its place came theological mysticism. One of the consequences of this was to draw him further apart from his wife, Natalya Reshetovskaya, who had stuck by him and given him as much support as she could, but she was strictly orthodox – a successful chemistry lecturer and brilliant pianist – with no transcendental thoughts nor beliefs in strength through suffering. She came to accept that it was necessary to divorce Alexander partly because they were on different planes and partly because otherwise she would get no promotion in her work; and Alexander felt he had to agree.

Another change to come to him was an intensifying in his determination to become a writer. He had much to say and was becoming aware of literary abilities. But he had to be cautious. The authorities disapproved of writing; it was

---

1 Inspired by the scripture: 'whosoever will save his life shall lose it and whosoever shall lose it for my sake shall find it.' (Matthew 16–25)

banned and practising it might lead to heavy penalties. So all he could do was to jot down words on odd bits of paper which he then burned after memorising what was written on them. Altogether he was to commit to memory some 12,000 lines. At first he composed mainly poetry, but later he changed his tune. He had a message for mankind, to expose man's inhumanity to man and to stress the evils inherent in totalitarianism (based on repression, mendacity and reliance on prison labour).

In 1953, after four years in the army and eight in prison, he was released. No matter that at first he was in perpetual exile in Kok-Terek, a dim outpost in barren Kazakhstan, with restrictions on what he could do and where he could go, and his home no more than a ramshackle shed with earthen floor and leaking roof and a bed contrived out of boxes. In time he was to find something more habitable and a job as a teacher. 'Beautiful exile', he declared, and his happiness was enhanced when within three weeks came news of the death of Stalin, the mass murderer still regarded by some Russians as their saviour with people weeping in the streets at the thought of his departure.

Suffering for Solzhenitsyn had not come to an end. Once again he was diagnosed for cancer and came near to death; but again, miraculously, he survived and was ready for the next stage.

This came with the rise to power of Nikita Khruschev and in 1956 his denunciation of Stalin. This led to Solzhenitsyn being pardoned and freed from exile, and it being declared that what he had written 'did not constitute proof of a crime' (for which he had been imprisoned for eight years).

His freedom was complete.

His writing could now come out into the open. As an author he was unknown with a pile of unpublished works; but words continued to pour from him, and he had in mind a project to which he attached special importance. He wanted to bring home to Russian people and the world at large how monstrously unjust and inhumane was the treatment of prisoners in forced labour camps. This he intended to do by describing in detail one day in the life of a typical prisoner, a brave thing to do, as the NKVD might come down on him heavily, and he would be back in prison; but he was determined to do it; it had to be done. The writing of it came fluently; in forty days it was finished. But what next?

Aware of the dangers of publication, in 1961 he took the plunge and *One Day in the Life of Ivan Denisovich* was submitted to Alexander Tvardovsky, editor of *Novy Mir*, a prominent literary magazine. Tvardovsky hadn't seen anything like it for a long time. Russian literature then was at a low ebb, heartless and stereotyped, and here was something stirring and vibrant. It seemed to him that the work was a major literary discovery. Copies were spread around in the following years and it was to come to the notice of Nikita Khruschev who was interested by it, as it would be an instrument in his de-Stalinisation campaign, and he ordered twenty-three copies to be circulated among the Presidium of the Party. Details of how it was received there are not known, but it is probable that there was a sharp clash between the liberal minded and the old timers, the doctrinaires, determined to hold fast to dogma and despotism. And so it came about that the unheard of scribbler, recently out of gaol, found himself a bone of contention at the centre of a power struggle in the Kremlin. It was a perilous position; he was on a knife edge.

For a time Khruschev prevailed, declaring that his book would 'clear up many things and tell the truth to the people.' Given his way it is probable that he would have gone further and set up a monument in Moscow in memory of 'comrades who fell victim to arbitrary power.' He was even contemplating abolishing censorship, but the forces against him were too powerful, and he felt it necessary to show that his policy of liberalism was paying off and that he was a strong and masterly leader, which led him to become involved in a rash and abortive venture in Cuba. This was a serious blow to his reputation and it became necessary to go slow on liberalism.

In 1964, Khruschev was forced into retirement, and his place as head of the government was taken by the hardliner Leonid Brezhnev, who was to hold on to office until he died eighteen years later, when he was succeeded by Yuri Andropov, head of KGB. Liberation from Communism was not to come yet.

With the downfall of Khruschev and the accession of Brezhnev, the fortunes of Solzhenitsyn were to take a turn for the worse. In 1964 he was denied the Lenin Prize for Literature and in 1969 he was expelled from the USSR Union of Writers. He was not, however, to retire into obscurity. He continued to fight on behalf of ex-prisoners like himself who had suffered injustice and cruelty, determined to remain their spokesman.

Of course, the NKVD was watching him closely. In earlier days it could soon have disposed of him, but as he had now become a figure of world renown it had to be wary. Drastic treatment might have wide repercussions, especially when in 1970 he was awarded the Nobel Prize for Literature (for 'the ethical force with which he pursued the indispensable tradition of Russian literature'), a prize he felt unable to collect in Stockholm for fear of not being allowed back into Russia.

For a time he was unmolested by the NKVD, but when it became known that he was engaged in writing an account of its history and methods (subsequently to become known as *The Gulag Archipelago*), action was taken. In 1974 he was arrested and sent into exile.

By then there had been changes in his personal circumstances. He had soon remarried Natalya Reshetovskaya, who stated that he was the only person with whom she had ever been seriously in love. But it was not to be plain sailing. They were in different political camps: Solzhenitsyn on the side of reform and Natalya in favour of the status quo. These were to diverge further with the publication of *One Day in the Life of Ivan Denisovich* and further still in 1972 when Solzhenitsyn pronounced himself a convert to Christianity and committed himself to the Russian Orthodox Church, while Natalya remained steadfastly atheist. In effect the remarriage had broken down but did not finally come to an end until divorce in 1973 when Solzhenitsyn was fifty-five. By then he had become closely associated with Natalya Svetlova (to become known as Alya), a lady of charm, beauty and great competence – also a fervent disciple of Solzhenitsyn both spiritually and politically. As soon as Solzhenitsyn's divorce became absolute they married, and she accompanied him into exile in Switzerland with three sons who had been born in quick succession – Yermolai, Ignat and Stepan.

In Switzerland, Solzhenitsyn found much that was agreeable – beautiful scenery, freedom from arrest and great resources for research. While there he wrote a highly controversial book, *Lenin in Zurich* which was to discredit Lenin's reputation. He had survived the denunciation of Stalin and was still regarded by many in Russia as sacrosanct. Solzhenitsyn was able to find evidence of his nefarious and treasonable dealings with German financiers during the First World War which led to his being transported in a sealed train from Zurich to St. Petersburg.

After a stay in Switzerland of three years, Solzhenitsyn and his family made a move to the United States. There he was to find himself not wholly welcome. The American government at that time was bent on détente with Russia, which he regarded as a betrayal of dissidents there, and his unremitting hostility to Communism was an embarrassment.

It was marked that he was not invited to the White House and was kept at a distance. There were even some who suspected him of Fascist tendencies – he who had borne arms against the Nazis for three years and been imprisoned for eight years for his opposition to totalitarianism. Suspicion of him increased when after a visit to Spain, still under the dictatorship of General Franco, he warned Spaniards against turning to democracy too quickly, stating, with some reason, that there was more freedom in Fascist Spain than in Communist Russia.

There were other issues too on which he was at variance with American opinion. In the Declaration of Independence of 1776 the founding fathers had promised life, liberty and the pursuit of happiness, but for him pursuit of happiness was not a priority, rather was spiritual growth for which suffering and self-limitation were necessary, and these were not in accordance with ever growing materialism. His mistrust of science was also held against him. Relativism, discovered by Albert Einstein in 1905, showed that truth and morality cannot be absolute but were relative to other considerations. This he could not accept. He believed firmly in absolute values.

One consequence of these differences was that Solzhenitsyn with his family was to withdraw to Vermont, a state in the north where, surrounded by a high fence, he distanced himself from outsiders and devoted himself to writing. His works were banned in Russia but had a widespread circulation in other countries, usually translated into over thirty languages. The publication of *The Gulag Archipelago* in Paris in 1973 caused turbulent sensation, particularly among leftist intellectuals who were aghast and mortified by its revelations, but still in many cases clinging to their belief that Russia was an earthly paradise. Other works published included semi-autobiographical prose-poems. In *Prussian Nights* he described the horrors of a victorious army taking revenge on defenceless citizens, murdering, raping and wantonly destroying churches, villages and farms. In *First Circle* he recalled his time in Marfino and dialectical arguments between prisoners of different persuasions. He was also to pour contempt on Russian writers who had given false pictures of labour camps, portraying them as humane and well disposed, making no mention of skeletal figures being worked to death in gruesome conditions.

Solzhenitsyn was to remain in his sanctuary in Vermont for eighteen years, but his heart was always in Russia and he had a strong ingrained confidence that one day he would return there with Communism overturned and beneficial democracy set up. How beneficial he was to come to doubt. His faith was shaken somewhat by a visit to England in 1976.

England at that time was in the throes of the so-called Permissive Society. Laws were being relaxed in such matters as divorce, abortion and homosexuality. Old principles and ideas were being ridiculed and flouted. Youth was feeling oppressed and unliberated from outdated notions and conventions, and was venting its discontent in noisy and flamboyant demonstrations (demos), sit-ins (sometimes lie-ins), raffish behaviour and outlandish appearance.[2] Protest and unorthodoxy were the order of the day.[3]

The Church of England was in retreat, lavishing sympathy on the protesters, some ministers seeming to have more affinity with Communism than with the Gospels; the 'Red Dean', Dr. Hewlett Johnson, from the pulpit of Canterbury Cathedral was exalting 'the glorious social experiment taking place in the Soviet Union', notwithstanding it was a sworn foe of Christianity and bent on its extinction.

---

2   Men's hair was becoming longer as women's skirts became shorter.

3   Middle-class agitators might have heeded the words of housewives in a poor part of London who sang out: 'Name your mercies. Count them one by one and it will surprise you how much the Lord hath done.'

For these movements Solzhenitsyn had little sympathy. Truth to him was absolute and it seemed that democracy was devolving into depravity. He was not in favour of the cult of youth, it not being 'in the natural order of things that those who are youngest with least experience of life should be the greatest influence in the life of society.' He came away from England with the thought that English democracy was no model for Russia when it was rid of Communism. His view of England, however, was unduly pessimistic. Materialism might be spreading, but all was not 'change and decay' (*The English Hymnal*).

Everyday life was carrying on with 'its daily stage of duty run' (ibid) – in offices, schools, farms, hospitals. For most, existence was on an even keel. Millions from all over the world were wanting to come and live in England's 'green and pleasant land' (*Jerusalem* by William Blake).

In Vermont in his sixties Solzhenitsyn was content, mainly engaged in writing but devoting time to the education of his three sons which he was determined should be of the best. He was an inspired teacher, not sombre and heavy handed but engaging and vivid with a lively wit and sense of humour. Unexpectedly he was to send his eldest son, Yermolai, to Eton for two years, which was to prove successful and enjoyable. His middle son, Ignat, proved to be a musical prodigy, playing a Beethoven piano concerto at the age of twelve and he went to the Purcell School of Music in Hertfordshire.

Life for Solzhenitsyn in Vermont might have been peaceful, but he could not but be troubled by what he heard from outside. Materialism was spreading far and wide, superseding spiritual values. He was always to take a stand against this, maintaining that life with only physical pleasures was mean and purposeless and brought no lasting satisfaction; but it was being borne in on him that he was swimming against the tide, and he wondered sometimes if western decadence was as bad as eastern despotism.

His love of Russia was always with him and he was convinced that he was destined to return there, and in the mid nineteen-eighties it seemed that the time for this might be arriving. When Leonid Brezhnev died in 1982 he was succeeded as General Secretary of the Communist Party first by Yuri Andropov and on his death a year later by Konstantin Chernenko, colourless hardliners; but in 1985 they were followed by Mikhail Gorbachev, a man of a different hue – broad-minded, charismatic and realistic, bringing with him glasnost (openness) and perestroika (reconstruction). He realised that since the election of Ronald Reagan as United States President in 1980 Russia was losing the arms race with America, and that Communism was on the way out. He was anxious to do a deal and Reagan was ready for this and with support from Margaret Thatcher, prime minister of Britain since 1979, they could do business, and détente became a reality. Events then were to come thick and fast: in 1989 there were the first signs of a major break-up in the Soviet empire in east Europe with serious revolts in Poland and Czechoslovakia once Russian dominance of their countries was withheld. Also the Berlin Wall was broken down, and in 1990 East and West Germany were united. In Russia there were power struggles between different factions resulting in Gorbachev being deposed in 1991, and Boris Yeltsin, an even stronger anti-Communist being elected as President of the newly formed Russian Republic. It was the end of the USSR, the Union of Soviet Socialist Republics.

Amidst these dramas Solzhenitsyn's Russian citizenship was restored. He had become something of a legend and warring parties were seeking his support, but this he was reluctant to give; he did not want to belong to any party right or left. He had an invitation from the Russian prime minister to visit him as his personal guest, but this he politely declined. He was not yet ready to return and made it clear that he would not do so until all Russians were free to read his books. In Vermont he was engrossed in completing what he considered to be his most important work, *The Red Wheel*, an exhaustive account of the Bolshevik revolution. But he was preparing to leave and finally was to go in 1994 at the age of seventy-six and after twenty years in exile.

His journey to Moscow was accompanied by much ceremony (which the BBC had purchased the sole right to cover). He decided not to go by direct flight but by train across the vast expanse of the continent, beginning at Vladivostok, the Russian seaport in the Pacific; the place where he first landed, Magdalen, had once been the site of a forced labour camp. Along the route he was greeted with enthusiasm and gifts, but in Moscow there was opposition. There were those who saw him as a relic of a bygone age with unfashionable and outdated views. Addicted to consumerism, they did not want to hear that acquisitiveness and gratification of every desire regardless of moral considerations led to an empty life, and a living death. They were set in their ways and not to be distracted from them. Communism was dead, and they did not need him to tell them so. He was, therefore, an irrelevance.[4] There were of course those too who looked on him as a prophet with glad tidings and hope and loved him dearly, but these were outnumbered by those on the sidelines who respected and revered him but paid only lip service, ready to praise his works if not to read them, and then to lapse into their materialist ways.

Solzhenitsyn was aware of this hostility and apathy and not unduly surprised by it. He knew what he was up against. He had of course no thoughts of being silenced, to do so

---

4   No more than what one called 'a provincial schoolteacher'.

would be a betrayal of his divine mission, but he did decide to rely on writing rather than speaking. And so he and Alya went again into seclusion in a large house in a wooded area outside Moscow, and there he set to work writing but making few public appearances. In the years that followed, his moods varied from dejection to occasional bouts of optimism. He could not but be deeply disappointed in the new Russia that had emerged since the fall of Communism. There were few signs of the 'grassroot' democracy which he had found in Switzerland and he was far removed from the Russia of Boris Yeltsin in which each man was out for what he could get and in rivalry rather than co-operation with his neighbour – a society in which popular tastes had been vulgarised, people preferring soap opera and sitcoms rather than Chekov and Turgenev. In his semi-seclusion he was to steer clear of the political arena and concentrate his efforts on the denigration of materialism and urging a spiritual revival. His aim was a return to the Russia of pre-revolutionary Communism but he knew in his heart of hearts that this was impossible. He who had had such a vital role in the downfall of Nazism and Communism could not prevail against consumerism.

He hoped, however, that he might still have some influence and that his ideas might take root. Mixed with despondency came rays of light. He liked to consider himself an optimist. He had reason to be. It was a miracle that he had survived. Had he not twice recovered from cancer when everyone else had written him off? And had he not returned triumphantly from an exile which was supposed to be permanent? He had hopes that he might still not be neglected, and was always driving home his main point that Russia's ills were due to God being forgotten and, as he put it, that godlessness led to the Gulag. He held out some notes of good cheer. He insisted that old age was not a path downward but rather a movement up. On one point he was definite – that there was life after death which was just a peaceful transition, only a stage, some might say even a liberation. The soul has continuation and lives on.

Incredibly he was to live on until 2008 when he died on 3 August just short of his ninetieth birthday. Few have shown such courage and strength of mind. The influence of his writings has been unique.

ACKNOWLEDGEMENTS

As an essayist rather than a historian, my sources have been secondary. I have left research to others. Of the greatest value has been *Intellectuals* by Paul Johnson (Weidenfeld and Nicolson, 1988). It was this book that I found fascinating and which has been my main guide and inspiration. Other sources have been the long and scholarly biography of William Tyndale by David Daniell (Yale, 1994). I made use of a briefer and more accessible biography by Melvyn Bragg (SPCK, 2017). Other books of help have been the biography of Thomas Paine by W.A. Speck (Pickering & Chatto, 2013), and Adrian Desmond's biography of Charles Darwin (Penguin, 2009) as well as Darwin's autobiography (Norton, 1958).

In writing this book I have had invaluable help from Claire Wingfield (Editorial and Literary Consultant), book designer and typesetter Dan Prescott (Couper Street Type Co.) and Delia Caple (Citysec International). I am also greatly indebted to my cousin Priscilla Baines who has been of help in many ways, tracing sources and fetching books from the London Library whose staff has, as always, been patient and cooperative.

INDEX

Adams, John 19
Animal Farm 90
Anna Karenina 61
Andropov, Yuri 106, 111
Antwerp 10, 11
Aragon, Catherine of 8

Barnaby Rudge 22
Beagle, H.M.S. 34–42
Beerbohm, Max 51
Behr, Sonya 58
Bernhardt, Sarah 51
Black Death 3
Black, Dora 70
Blair, Eric 75
Boleyn, Anne 8–9
Bonaparte, Napoleon 29
Bonneville, Nicolas de 28
Boston Tea Party 20
Brezhnev, Leonid 111
British Museum 46–47
Burke, Edmund 22, 30

Catiline 52
Cambridge University 34, 39, 66
Campaign for Nuclear Disarmament 65, 72
Castro, Fidel 73, 97
Caxton, William 4
Childhood 58
Charles V 6
Cheetham, James 31
Chernenko, Konstantin 111
Chertkov, Vladimir 62
Clement VII, Pope 8, 11
Conditions of the Working Class in England 47
Conquest of Happiness 68
Cologne 5
Communist Manifesto, The 45, 46, 48
Confessions 17
Corday, Charlotte 26
Cromwell, Thomas 9

Cuban missile crisis 73
Curzon, Lord 51

Danton, Georges 27
Darwin, Charles 33–43
Deism 27
Diderot, Denis 17
Disraeli, Benjamin 40
Doll's House, A 53, 55
Down and Out in Paris and London 79
Dudley, Helen 70
Dundas, Henry 25

Edinburgh University 33
Edward III 4
Engels, Friedrich 47
English Hymnal, The 110
Erasmus, Desiderius 3, 5
Eton 75, 110

Finch, Edith 70
First Circle 109
Fitzroy, Robert 34–35, 38, 42

Galapagos Islands 36–38
Gandhi, Mahatma 76
Gaunt, John of 4
Geneva 13
Girondists 26
Gollancz, Victor 79, 86, 91
Gorbachev, Mikhail 111

Greene, Nathanael 21
Gulag Archipelago, The 106, 108
Gutenberg, Johannes 4

Hamilton, Alexander 30
Hedda Gabler 53
Henry VIII 6–9
Henslow, Rev. John 34, 39
History of Western Philosophy 68
Homage to Catalonia 87
Human Knowledge 68
Hume, David 17
Huxley, Thomas 41, 42
Hychyns, William ix, 2

Ibsen, Henrik 51–55

Jacobins 26, 28
James I 1
Jefferson, Thomas 29–30
Jerome, Saint 5
Jerusalem 110
Johnson, Paul 18, 46, 115

Kant, Immanuel 16
Kapital, Das 48, 50, 102
Kazakhstan 104
Keep the Aspidistra Flying 78
Kok-Terek 104
Khruschev, Nikita 104–106

Laski, Harold 86, 91
Lenin in Zurich 107
Lenin Prize for Literature 106
Levasseur, Thérèse 14–15
Leo V, Pope 6
Lollards 4
London School of Economics 72, 86
Louis XVI 21, 26
Lubyanka 102
Luther, Martin 4–6
Lutheranism 6

Macmillan, Harold 73
Magdalen College 2
Malleson, Constance 70
Marat, Jean Paul 26
Marfino 103, 109
Master Builder, The 53
Martin, Kingsley 86
Marx, Karl 45–50, 74, 93, 102
Monroe, James 28
Montaigu, Comte de 14
More, Sir Thomas 6, 8
Morrell, Ottoline 70
Muggeridge, Malcolm 76

Nineteen Eighty-Four 91–92
NKVD 102, 105, 106
Nobel Prize for Literature 106

One Day in the Life of Ivan Denisovich 105
Origin of Species by Natural Selection 40
Orwell, George 16, 75–93
O'Shaughnessy, Eileen 80
Oxford University 2, 3, 5, 10, 41, 42

Paine, Thomas 19–31
Peasants' Revolt 4
Peer Gynt 53
Pentateuch, The 10
Phillips, Henry 10–11
Poyntz, Thomas 10
Pollitt, Harry 83, 85–86
Price, Richard 22
Prussian Nights 108

Reagan, Ronald 111
Red Wheel, The 112
Reflections on Revolution in France 23
Reshetovskaya, Natalya 102–103, 106
Rights of Man, The 23–25, 31
Road to Wigan Pier 80
Robespierre, Maximilien 13, 27
Roosevelt, Theodore 19
Rostov 101

Rousseau, Jean-Jacques
   13–18, 61, 74, 98
Russell, Bertrand   65–74

Saint Paul's Cathedral   6
Sartre, Jean-Paul   95–99
Schiller, Friedrich   17
Schoenman, Ralph   72
Shakespeare, William   2, 54, 55
Shelley, Percy Bysshe   17
Shrewsbury   33
Smillie, Bob   86
Social Contract, The   16, 17
Solzhenitsyn, Alexander   101–114
Spence, Patricia   70
Stokesley, John   10
Svetlova, Natalya   107

Thatcher, Margaret   111
Thetford   19, 31
Thoreson, Susannah   52
Tolstoy, Leo   57–63
Towton   2
Treaty of Amiens   30
Trevelyan, G. M.   43
Trotsky, Leon   84
Tvardovsky, Alexander   105
Tyndale, William   ix, 1–12

Utopia   6

Vilvorde   11
Vladivostok   112
Voltaire   13, 16
Vulgate, The   5

Walsh, Sir John   3
War and Peace   58, 61
Wars of the Roses   2
Washington, George   27–31
Waynflete, William   2
Wedgwood, Emma   39
Wedgwood, Josiah   34
Wellington College   75
Whitall, Alys   68
Wilberforce, Samuel   41
Wild Duck   53
Wittenberg Castle   4
Wittgenstein, Ludwig   68
Wolsey, Thomas   2, 6, 8
Wycliffe, John   3, 4

Yasnaya Polyana   57, 61
Yeltsin, Boris   111, 113

Born in 1926, Mark Hichens is a biographer, historian and retired teacher. His works include: *Oscar Wilde's Last Chance: The Dreyfus Connection* ('Hichens's narrative is fresh. He writes with clarity, pace, wisdom and wry humour' THE SPECTATOR), *Prime Ministers' Wives* ('Well written and well researched' SUNDAY TELEGRAPH) and *Abdication: The Rise and Fall of Edward VIII*.

otp

52 Dates for Writers
Claire Wingfield

This essential creative writing guide will take you away from your desk, to return with new ideas, fresh insight, better writing skills, and a renewed passion for your novel. It's suitable for both those who are seeking tried-and-tested strategies for revising a novel draft, and those who would like to improve their understanding of the writer's craft – to learn how to write a book that truly satisfies readers – and generate a store of ideas before starting to write a novel.

Each of the 52 activities for writers to get out and do – from climbing a hill to visiting a favourite café, from sampling a new mode of transport to taking part in a hi-tech treasure hunt – is accompanied by an essay on an aspect of the writer's craft, and practical exercises to help with writing or revising your novel.

Including examples from well-known novels, and a chapter on editing your work, '52 Dates for Writers' covers both the craft and business of writing – from how to write better dialogue and revamp your storyline, to how to write your synopsis like a pro and understand your market.

£7.99
ISBN 978-0-9575279-1-1

www.ingramcontent.com/pod-product-compliance
Lightning Source LLC
Chambersburg PA
CBHW071353080526
44587CB00017B/3088